A Memoir of Home, War and
Finding Refuge

Biruta's Story

A Memoir of Home, War and Finding Refuge, Biruta's Story

Published by
Hardes Press
San Diego, CA

Cover and Interior design by Olga Singer of Simply Two Design
Map by Charles Hardes

Copyright 2020
ISBN: 978-0-578-73825-3

Library of Congress Cataloging-In-Publication Data available upon request.

Grateful acknowledgment is made to the family of
Latvian artist **Arvids Drone (1918-2006)** for the use of his original oil painting,
Druva, **1957,** on the book's cover.

HARDES ❧ PRESS

A Memoir of Home, War and
Finding Refuge

Biruta's Story

Lilita Zvejnieks Hardes

www.lhardes.com

Dedication

To Biruta, and her family

Karlis Treumans (Opa),
Elsa Riesbergs (Mother),
Hermanis Riesbergs (Father).
Emma Ozolins Treumans (Oma),
Biruta and Elga Riesbergs. Circa 1935

Maija Riesbergs
Circa 1950

TABLE OF CONTENTS

TABLE OF CONTENTS
contniued

Prologue

❦

Latvia

Latvia, Lithuania, and Estonia are three small countries located north of Poland on the Baltic Sea. Latvia's landmass is about half the size of Greece, and it is positioned between Estonia to the north and Lithuania to the south. Latvia and Estonia share eastern borders with Russia, and the three Baltic states share their western maritime borders with Sweden.

During the middle ages, German barons and overlords governed Latvia. In the 1700 and 1800s, Russian tsars took over but allowed the German nobility and their local religious governments to stay. Germany and Russia had strong influences on Latvia's culture and history. Latvia has its own language, but Russian and German are also spoken.

In 1917, the Russian revolution dismantled the tsarist monarchy. At the end of World War I, the roles of Germany and Russia were diminished across Europe. Their loss of power facilitated Latvia's independence in 1918. It remained an independent country for the 22 years between the two world wars. By 1928 Josef Stalin had become a brutal dictator in Russia. The autonomous nations of Latvia, Lithuania, and Estonia, positioned at Russia's doorstep, kept a watchful eye on their neighbor.

My story begins in 1939 when nearly two million inhabitants lived in peace and prosperity in the sovereign country of Latvia. I was born in 1930 and spent my childhood in the capital city of Riga near the Eastern shores of the Baltic Sea.

NORTHERN EUROPE 1939

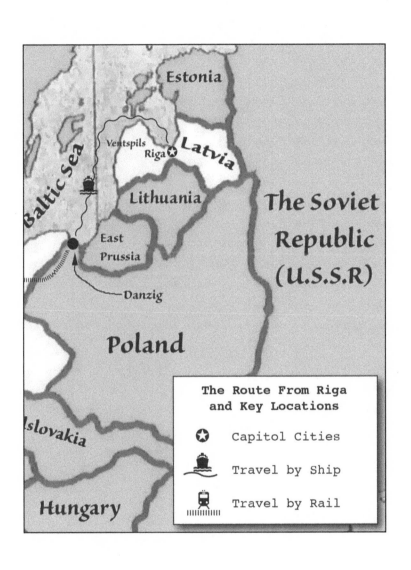

CHAPTER 1

Alexander Heights, Riga, Latvia | 1939

"We are not makers of history; we are made by history." [1]

I had no say over the time or place in history in which I was born. Likewise, I had no sway over the politics of the world which played out while I was growing up in Latvia. Both realities profoundly influenced who I am and shaped the story of my life.

I like to shock people by telling them I grew up in a mental institution. It is true only because Father and Mother both worked as psychiatrists at Alexander Heights, a state hospital in Latvia's capital city of Riga. Their employment benefits included housing on the hospital grounds. My fraternal twin sister, Elga, and I were born in 1930. We lived at Alexander Heights the first nine years of our lives with my parents, Drs. Hermanis and Elsa Riesbergs.

My family lived in the main hospital building, which sat at the center of Alexander Heights. It was an imposing three-story structure and took up almost an entire city block. Our family resided in one of two first floor physician apartments. The director's residence and the administrative offices were also on the first floor. Mother worked in the bacteriologic lab on the second floor. The third floor housed a patient ward. The top two stories were off-limits to Elga and me.

We entered our apartment through a long hallway that stretched the length of our floor. A small foyer opened to an ample living and dining room. Off of the dining room was the kitchen, and on the other side was my parents' bedroom and a bathroom. Elga and I slept in the den, which served as our bedroom. We were the only children living in the building. Besides being my twin, Elga was my primary playmate, and we were the closest of friends.

The Daugava River flowed through the heart of Riga and fed into the Baltic Sea. The hospital at Alexander Heights was in northcentral Riga, near a serene channel of the river. A concrete wall completely enclosed the entire complex. In addition to the hospital buildings, inside the walls was a picturesque landscape. It included manicured lawns, a fishpond, and a thick grove of oak trees with a gazebo. Flowering gardens sloped toward the river channel. Next to the gardens was an operational farm.

Elga and I explored and played for hours on the protected, park-like grounds. We often pretended we were part of Prince Alexander's court. He was the Russian Tsar from the 1800s for whom Alexander Heights was named. It stirred our imaginations to think we lived on the very property that once hosted visiting Russian tsars and royalty.

Our maternal grandparents, who we called Oma and Opa, lived just a few miles from Alexander Heights and visited us often. Much to our delight, Elga and I spent our summers with them. They were like second parents to us.

During the school term, Christina, a cousin of Father's, worked as our housekeeper and watched us after school. Father's younger brother, Oskars, worked in the business offices at Alexander Heights. He lived in a cottage on the grounds with my aunt and two cousins. Surrounded by family, I felt my life was perfect. Never did I imagine that things could be any different.

～

Evenings were my favorite time of day. After a family dinner, Elga and I would join our parents in the living room. Mother would ease onto the sofa, pick up her sewing basket, and pull out her latest cross-stitch project. Father sat across from her in his overstuffed chair and turned on the radio beside him on a stand. Retrieving a slim silver case from his inside jacket pocket and taking out a cigarette, he lit it for his after-dinner smoke.

Inhaling on his cigarette and closing his eyes, Father listened to classical music playing softly in the background. Tchaikovsky's symphonies were his favorites. As he exhaled, a wispy cloud of smoke swirled over his head as he set down the cigarette in a glass ashtray next to him. He reached for the evening paper and began to read. Elga and I sat on a rug at our parents' feet, listening to the soothing music and entertaining ourselves with our dolls and stuffed animals.

When it was time for bed, Elga and I stalled our parents by stretching every last possible moment with them. We delayed putting away our toys and took our time putting on our nightgowns and washing up. Each evening, either Mother or Father tucked us into bed and read or told us a story. Above all we loved to hear the stories when they were young.

"What story do you want to hear tonight?" Mother asked, entering our room and settling into a chair between us.

From previous stories, we learned Mother had primarily been raised as an only child. She lost her only sister to an early childhood illness. Because of it, Mother remained especially close to Oma and Opa.

"I want to hear how you became a doctor," Elga said.

"And I want to hear how you met Father," I added.

"I think you each could tell those stories yourselves by now," Mother said with a smile. "All right, then. Ever since I was a little girl, like you two, my father stressed the importance of getting a good education and learning a skill that could be used anywhere in the world. I loved the sciences and studied hard. When I was 17, I got accepted into medical school."

"But how did you and Father meet?" I asked, even though I knew the answer.

Mother smiled and continued, "I first met him in medical school, but he was a year ahead of me, and when he graduated, we lost contact."

"Then how did you get back together again?"

"Well, when I finished school, I was hired at Alexander Heights. I didn't know your father was already working here. We got reacquainted and became close friends. Over time, we fell in love and got married. As new doctors at a state hospital, we worked hard to pay off our medical school debts. Father took a second job at the state prison, where he still consults. A year later, the two of you came along and have been worth every penny," Mother said as she tweaked our noses. "Now it's getting late, and you need your sleep. Oma will be coming for you in the morning."

Other nights, but not as often, Father would tuck us into bed. He told us stories about growing up on a farm in a region of Latvia called Vidzeme, a few hours north of Riga. He had four brothers, two older and two younger. In the Latvian tradition, his oldest brother inherited the farm. After Father's country education ended in the eighth grade, he and his other brothers were sent off to the city for additional schooling. Father himself was a twin, but his brother died in infancy, and he had never known him.

Sometimes Father would read books or recite Latvian poetry and rhymes to us in his silly singsong voice. All the same, each of our parents similarly ended our nighttime routine. They said our bedtime prayers with us and kissed us on the cheek before turning out the lights and leaving the room. Satisfied that all was right with my world, I fell asleep.

❧

Wake up, Elga," I shouted and pulled off her bed covers. "I want to go down to the farm to see the animals. We haven't been there in weeks!"

Our school term had just ended, and it was our first day of summer vacation.

I threw open the curtains. Rays of light filtered through a canopy of leaves on a large chestnut tree just outside our window. Scattered sunbeams danced across the floor. The tree's branches were heavy with fragrant blossoms, and a breeze blew the sweet smell into the room. I drew in a deep breath holding in the scent. The tree marked our seasons.

In the fall, Elga and I collected the chestnuts that fell from the tree to make tiny baskets for our dolls. During the winter months, when the tree limbs were bare, we'd gaze out the window down to the frozen river channel to watch men hauling blocks of ice into an ice house nearby.

Elga stretched lazily, brushed the sleep from her eyes, and sat up in her bed.

"Okay, Biruta," she yawned. "Let's find someone to take us."

The farm stood on a lower portion of Alexander Heights near the river channel. Some of the healthier patients tended the horses, pigs, rabbits, and guinea pigs housed there. We were only permitted to go there with supervision. We threw on our play clothes and raced to find an adult.

Speeding down the hall, the aroma of fresh-baked bread greeted our noses. In the kitchen, we saw Christina, our housekeeper, standing over the cutting board, slicing a loaf.

"Christina, can we go to the farm?" my sister asked with a pleading whine. "We want to see the horses."

Elga was 45 minutes older than me. She often felt it gave her the authority to take charge.

"I want to see the other animals, too!" I objected.

"I know," Elga said, looking at me and then turning her gaze to Christina, "Anyway, can we go?"

"You'll need to ask your mother," Christina replied. "Why don't you girls sit down and have some breakfast? Your mother should be on break soon. You can ask then if she is available to take you. I have chores to do."

"No, thanks, we're not hungry. We need to find Mother," Elga said.

She ran from the kitchen, grabbing a slice of warm bread, munching on it on her way out. Christina frowned as she watched her leave.

Following Elga's lead, I grabbed a slice too and ran

after her. Scurrying out of the apartment, we finished eating our bread and raced down the hallway. We skidded to a stop mid-corridor at the business office.

Flinging the door open and dashing inside, we panted to the secretary, "Where's Mother?"

"Girls, you need to quiet down," she said, throwing us an irritated look. "Your mother is in the lab and isn't due for her break for another 20 minutes."

Hearing that Mother was unavailable, we hung our heads, trying to decide what to do next. Suddenly, Elga yanked my arm backward.

"C'mon, Biruta. Let's go outside."

As we left the office, Elga called over her shoulder to the secretary, "Tell Mother we'll be out front."

Struggling to keep my balance while Elga pulled me into the hallway, I added, "Tell her it's important. We want to go to the farm."

The secretary raised her eyebrows and with a flip of her hand, signaled us to leave.

"Do you think she'll let Mother know?" I complained as we stepped out into the sunshine.

Elga shrugged her shoulders and sprawled out on the warm green grass while I collapsed onto the stairs. We remained silent for several moments.

A huge sigh escaped from Elga, "Now, what'll we do?"

I stood up and strolled across the lawn, dragging my feet over to the fishpond. I watched the fish gliding by and picked up a small branch at the foot of the pond, swirling it on top of the water.

"Elga, remember how we used to try to catch these fish with a bent stickpin on a string?" I giggled.

"Yeah, but I don't feel like doing that now. I want to go to the farm," Elga lamented as she walked toward me. "Where is Mother? Why isn't she here yet?"

Then we heard a familiar voice calling from nearby. "Biruta, Elga, where have you been? I went to the apartment looking for you. Oma is coming today."

Oma? Elga and I looked at each other with eyes wide open. Going to grandmother's was much more exciting than going to the farm.

"I can't believe you girls have forgotten," Mother said as she approached us. "Hurry! You'll need to get your things for the day. Father and I will come over to Oma's and Opa's after work."

Shooing us back to the apartment, she added, "Oma will be here any minute, and you won't be ready. It's getting warm, and she was planning to take you to the lake."

The lake! It was mid-morning, and already I felt the sun's rays warming my face and the back of my neck. The lake was near our grandparents' house and was one of our favorite summer spots to cool down. Elga and I raced ahead of Mother, hurrying to our room to gather our swimming items for an afternoon at the beach.

Mother waited for us and then exclaimed, "Quickly, girls! I need to get back to the lab. Oma should be here soon."

We rushed out to give Mother a quick hug and kiss before she left to go back to work. Elga and I grabbed our things and went outside to watch for the first signs of Oma coming through the front gates of Alexander Heights.

A few minutes later, I spied her first. "There she is!"

Elga and I ran toward her, shouting, "Oma, here we are!"

When we reached her, Oma teased, "I heard from a little birdie that you two had forgotten I was coming today. I guess I'll just have to go back home and go to the lake by myself."

"Oh no, Oma! We didn't mean to forget!" Elga cried out.

"We were thinking about the farm, and it slipped our minds," I said, looking down and kicking the ground with the heel of my shoe.

"Well, we have the whole summer ahead for adventures, but today, let's cool down by the lake before we melt," Oma chuckled with a twinkle in her eye. We stepped up our pace and skipped the rest of the way to our grandparents' house.

CHAPTER 2
Mezparks

The grounds at Alexander Heights were our playground, but Oma and Opa's house in Mezparks was our summer retreat. Elga and I stayed with them at the end of every school term. Mezparks, meaning "Forest Park," was only two miles from Alexander Heights. The neighborhood was densely wooded with the houses nestled among tall pine trees tucked away from the street. Some of my fondest memories were of my summers in Mezparks with Oma and Opa.

Elga and I delighted in our grandparents' two-story gingerbread bungalow. It was a modest home compared to some of the larger ones in the area, but it suited us well. We played in the two enclosed verandas flanking the house; a large one on one side and a smaller one on the other. The first floor included the kitchen, dining room, living room, and a small office for Opa. Two bedrooms were upstairs.

By the time Oma, Elga, and I reached our grandparents' home, we were perspiring from the walk. Like other houses in Mezparks, Oma and Opa's home was heavily shaded, keeping the indoors cool. Elga and I sprinted ahead, pushing the side door open. We ran into the kitchen, grabbing and gulping glasses of water for relief.

Setting our water glasses in the sink, Elga and I ran up the stairs to the bedrooms. One was Oma and Opa's, and the smaller bedroom was ours for the summer. In the center of our room was a wooden desk with single beds on either side. Anxious to start our summer, we threw our things onto the beds and hurried to change into our bathing suits to go to nearby Lake Kisezers.

The window above the small sofa on the opposite wall of our bedroom was open. It overlooked the yard and the forest of trees surrounding the home. Elga and I jumped onto the sofa and stuck our heads out the window, taking in long, deep breaths. The fresh scent of pine mingled in the air with the bread Oma had baked earlier that morning. I closed my eyes and inhaled to savor the smells. I heard the gentle whisper of the wind flowing through *Leila Priede*, the big pine tree Elga and I had named for our not-so-secret meeting place in the backyard.

"Isn't it great that summer is finally here?" I said in a dream-like trance.

"Yes," Elga replied, "but let's hurry and get to the lake."

We both raced downstairs to the kitchen. Eagerly awaiting us, Oma closed her picnic basket.

"I made some sandwiches and lemonade while you girls were upstairs. If you're ready, I think we should go."

Carrying our towels and floatation rings, Elga and I rushed for the door. Oma grabbed the picnic basket, and we headed for the lake.

From our grandparents' house, we followed a walkway for three or four blocks past the entrance to the zoo. The path to the lake was a short distance further. We came through the trees and saw the sandy shore of Lake Kisezers.

Elga spied some shorebirds and shouted, "Look, Oma, did you bring any food for the gulls?'

"Why yes," Oma said, digging through her basket and giving her a slice of stale bread. "This should keep the birds happy."

They both pinched off pieces of bread and threw them into the air, laughing as the gulls flew wildly around them, fighting for the crumbs.

Anxious to escape the heat, I slipped away. Grabbing a life ring and putting it around my waist, I waded out into the water. I began bouncing further from the shore into deeper water. Jumping too high, the life ring slipped down below my hips. I lost my balance and toppled over. The ring flipped me upside down, lifting my legs above me and holding my head underwater. Unable to breathe, I panicked as I struggled to kick free, but couldn't. In a matter of seconds, Oma and Elga heard my splashing and ran toward me through the water.

Oma snatched the ring from my legs. I put my feet on the sandy lake bottom, pushing up as hard as I could. I broke the surface of the water gasping for air, coughing, and sputtering. Seeing Oma, Elga, and the sky above them never felt so good. They each took one of my arms and helped me to shore. I gulped the air trying to refill my lungs. Oma threw a towel around me and held me close. She rubbed my arms and legs until my shivering subsided.

"Biruta, are you alright? You gave us quite a scare," Oma

said, her voice shaking. "Don't ever go out into the water alone again," she admonished.

"Yes," Elga said. "Or at least tell us when you're going in! What happened?"

"I was jumping too high and flipped over…"

"Oh my, it would have been terrible had Elga and I not been nearby. Thank goodness you're safe." Oma held me for several minutes until my breathing returned to normal.

Attempting to distract us, Oma asked if we were hungry and reached to open her picnic basket.

Elga and I each grabbed a sandwich and sat on the shore. The event was still fresh on our minds, and we ate in silence. After we finished eating, we began playing in the sand, building castles and moats and splashing in the shallows. Before long, the incident was forgotten.

We swam and stayed at the beach until the sun lowered on the horizon, and cool breezes brushed our newly sun-kissed skin. The sky turned deeper shades of pink and orange before we wandered back to our grandparents' home. The afternoon, however, was a reminder not to be lulled into a false sense of security.

～⚬✦⚬～

Our maternal grandmother, Oma, was born in 1881 and named Emma Amalia Jenny Lina Ozolins. At the tender age of six, her beloved father, in his early thirties, died of tuberculosis. In Riga in the late 1800s, Mikelis Ozolins had been a blacksmith shoeing horses and repairing ironwork. He also tinkered with making jewelry. He made a special charm for his eldest daughter, Emma, a miniature pair of blacksmith tongs that Oma still wore on a silver chain around her neck.

Emma's widowed mother, Marija, was heartbroken and unable to care for four children alone. She sent Emma, her oldest daughter, to live with her sister and brother-in-law, the Walters. Emma saw her mother and siblings regularly, but the Walters were in a better position to provide for her and her educational needs. Emma's uncle, Pastor Carl Walters, led the congregation at St. Peter's Church with its landmark steeple. It sat in the heart of the city on the cobblestoned streets of Old Town Riga Square and was originally built in 1209.

As Emma grew older, she played a significant role in the Walters' family. The family eventually grew to 12 children, and she helped care for them. Pastor Walters was originally from Germany, and German was spoken in their home. Emma became fluent in the language and trained to be a governess. At the tender age of 16, she left Latvia to be hired by a wealthy land baron in Ukraine. She cared for his children and taught them German.

Oma was a great storyteller. Elga and I often persuaded her to tell us stories about her days as a governess.

"Tell us again what it was like living with the baron and his family. Did they really treat you like royalty?"

"When I was a governess, they considered me a part of their family," Oma said, "and included me in all their social activities. I went to grand parties and dances at their estate. I had dark hair cascading down my back, reaching below my waist. Several handsome young men pursued me. I even refused the advances of a Russian aristocrat."

It was hard for Elga and me to imagine that Oma had been a dazzling debutante in her day. Now 58 years old, ancient to us, she was short in stature with fine lines beginning to crease her forehead and the corners of her eyes. Her hair was graying and no longer flowed down her back. It was neatly pinned in a bun at the nape of her neck. She still had a rosy complexion, sparkling eyes, and a ready smile which exuded her grandmotherly warmth. Good nature radiated from every inch of her. It was easy to see why she was so well-liked by young and old.

Our grandfather, Opa, was born Karlis Treumanns, Jr. in 1878. During Elga's and my summers at Mezparks, Opa often worked late as the head accountant at a bank in Riga. When he came home on summer evenings and hung up his hat, Elga and I ran to greet him. After dinner, if it was not too late and he wasn't too tired, we would plead for him to tell us about his youth as well.

"Sit down next to me, girls," Opa said as he patted the sofa cushions.

We settled in on either side of him as he put his arm around each of us.

"My father was a pub owner in Talsi, an area west of Riga. Early in my childhood, I would spend time after school at the pub," he said, pulling us in closer. "There was a small group of musicians who took an interest in me, and I liked being with them. I had an ear for music, and one of the musicians whittled a small flute for me out of a willow branch. It was the first instrument I ever had," he said as his voice trailed off, remembering the scene. "And you know how I still love music to this day."

As if on cue, Elga and I said in unison, "Opa, would you play something for us, please?"

Opa stood up, reaching for a small black case on top of the piano.

"Alright, tonight, I'll play, but you'll each need to learn an instrument yourselves soon."

He opened the case, assembled the sections of his silver flute with the gold mouthpiece, and put it to his lips to play. A tuneful melody floated out into the summer night. When he finished, Elga and I clapped our hands in delight. The flute was his favorite instrument, but he also played the piano, violin, and cello.

"Tomorrow night, girls, we start music lessons. Who wants to learn the piano, and who wants to learn the violin?" he asked.

"I want to learn the piano," I proclaimed.

In my mind, the piano was a more straightforward instrument. It was just a matter of placing your fingers on the right keys. The violin had to be tuned each time before it was played, and the fingers positioned precisely on each string to produce the right note. For once, Elga had no strong opinion, so my preference won out. Opa smiled and, over the summer months, taught each of us the magic of music on our chosen instruments.

The music in Oma and Opa's home was one of the reasons Elga and I loved being with them. Their house was always filled with the quiet happiness that music provided. It was a part of who they were and what had brought them together.

After Oma's year as a governess in Ukraine, she returned to the Walters home in Riga. Like most young people, she socialized with friends at each other's homes. Music was often at the core of these gatherings and was how my grandparents met. Oma had a beautiful, lilting singing voice, and Opa played accompaniment. It was a natural fit. They fell in love and married in 1902.

❧

Most summer mornings, I woke up to hear Oma's sweet singing voice floating up from the kitchen. She often went about her daily chores singing or humming German hymns or Latvian melodies. If I awoke first, I would stretch and lie in bed, putting my hands behind my head to listen. If Elga stirred, we looked at each other and smiled until the smells of breakfast pulled us from our beds.

After breakfast, Oma often gave us a short German lesson. In Latvia, it was almost a necessity to know a second language. Many people spoke German or Russian in addition to Latvian. When Oma and Opa went to school in the late 1800s, Latvian schools and universities were taught in German. When Elga and I started school, Latvian was used for all classes. Later in school, we also learned some English.

Because of Oma's and Opa's upbringing, Mother grew up speaking German more often than Latvian in their home. In medical school, Father and Mother learned Latin, the basis of several languages. Mother was adept at picking up new languages and knew some French and Russian as well. Father was most comfortable with Latvian, and we spoke it in our home at Alexander Heights.

Our summer German lessons with Oma consisted of learning phrases and platitudes of wisdom from her childhood.

When Elga and I wanted to pick flowers for Mother, Oma would tell us in German, "Flowers are not only to be picked, but also to beautify the garden."

When we played too aggressively and accidentally broke something, she shook her head and said, "Happiness and glass break easily."

However, our favorite German phrase was "Hans Wurst in allen gassen". The words themselves sounded so silly. The phrase translated to, "John Sausage (a commoner) in every alley". It was an insult to someone's ordinary qualities. Unknown to Oma, it became Elga's and my secret weapon.

The two boys next door, similar in age to us, didn't know any German. When they bothered us, we taunted them with the phrase, convulsing into fits of laughter. Although the boys didn't know what we were saying, they knew our words were unkind. They often ran to tattle on us to their mother, who told them not to play anymore with the mean girls across the yard.

A variety of other activities filled our summers in Mezparks. One morning, Elga and I were on knees with Oma in her garden in the backyard. We were pulling up beets, and several baskets were overflowing.

"Look at all of this!" Oma exclaimed. "We won't be able to use all of this ourselves. I've already given away so many to the neighbors. I think it's time for a trip to the zoo."

The zoo staff encouraged Oma to bring her over-abundance of vegetables to feed the animals. I jumped up, brushing the dirt from my knees and clapping my hands. From Oma and Opa's house, the zoo was just a short walk along the route to the lake.

Gathering up the beets and with baskets in hand, Elga and I all but ran to the zoo, trying not to spill them. We went with Oma to the buffalo pen, and from behind the fence, emptied our baskets into the feeding trough. We laughed to see such huge animals trotting over for their treat. They loved the sweet taste of beets and pushed and shoved each other aside to get to them.

"Biruta, look!" Elga shrieked. "They're slobbering all over each other!"

"Yuck!" I shouted at the disgusting sight.

We squealed with amusement to see the hungry beasts fighting at the trough and finishing every last beet.

With our task accomplished, Elga and I wiped tears of laughter from our faces. We strolled with Oma over to the monkey cages and laughed all over again to see them frolicking and chasing each other. Walking further down the path, we paused to watch the lions lazing in their grassy enclosure. Looking like giant housecats, one slowly got up and, with jaws wide open, let out a roar, startling us. Going to the zoo never ceased to entertain us.

⤝

In the quiet summer evenings, it was common for our parents to ride their bikes from Alexander Heights to Mezparks after work. Cars in Latvia were a luxury few could afford.

After dinner, Opa's musician friends often gathered at our grandparents' home. They played their instruments while Mother accompanied them on the piano. Elga and I loved to hear the music and see the adults enjoying their impromptu concerts. The music, singing, and laughter that drifted from the Oma's and Opa's home during those summer evenings warmed my heart and made me happy.

After the concert, the adults usually settled in with some light refreshments to talk about the topics of the day. Not wanting to miss out on anything, Elga and I often found a place on a braided rug on the floor close to our parents. We played quietly while listening to the adult conversation.

One late summer evening, the discussion took a somber turn. It was friendly and pleasant at first, but then tones became brusque. Stern looks replaced smiles. Not understanding the reason, I found myself clinging more tightly to one of my dolls.

Leaning forward in his chair, Father raised his voice, commanding the attention in the room.

"Have you heard the Russians and the Germans have signed a non-aggression agreement?"

Shaking his head in disapproval, Father reached over to tap the graying end of his cigarette into the ashtray next to him. Elga and I exchanged glances. We had never heard him so outspoken before.

One of Opa's friends swirled his drink staring into his glass.

"Yes, they call it the Molotov-Ribbentrop Agreement, and the Soviets and Nazis are surely up to no good."

With that declaration, he emptied his glass as if trying to drown his fears. The tension in the room only increased as everyone mulled over what he had said.

"The Soviets are always stirring something up," another musician friend chimed in. "Why Russia's Stalin and Germany's Hitler have signed an agreement is anybody's guess."

He lit a cigarette and continued, "But Latvia is now a part of the League of Nations, and I hear British and American ships are in the North Sea. Since our independence, our allies would never allow the Russians or Germans to occupy us again."

"I'm not sure the League of Nations can stop those godforsaken Russians," Opa said, shifting in his chair. "I don't trust Stalin for a minute. He's always wanted better access to the Baltic Sea. Remember, Leningrad is frozen in most of the winter. Our additional ports would provide those da...."

"Opa?" Oma, who had been silent throughout the

conversation, tilted her head in our direction and rose to go to the kitchen to refill the serving dishes.

Nodding, Opa continued, "...give the Russians an economic and military advantage. They've coveted our ports for centuries. Their armies far outnumber all the forces in the Baltics. We could never stop them without assistance."

Not understanding the adult discussion, I lost interest. Leaning over, I whispered to Elga, "Why don't we go upstairs to our room?"

She nodded to me, signaling okay. In school, we had learned about German and Russian influences in our country. I knew Latvians were fiercely proud of their 21 years of independence, but adult political discussions bored me. Elga seemed more interested in the evening's conversation. She hesitated before going to kiss our parents and grandparents goodnight and saying good-bye to their friends.

When we got up to our room, she initiated a power struggle in the play between our toys, deciding who should run the country.

Always the leader, Elga insisted, "I'll be the president, and you can be the vice-president."

Willing to keep the peace, I rolled my eyes and quietly played along.

❧

Summer flowed into autumn. Elga and I returned to our family's apartment at Alexander Heights and were back at school. In no time, winter was upon us, and the Christmas holiday approached. I had all but forgotten the adult concerns we had heard at the end of the summer. Like many children, I was eagerly awaiting Christmas.

"Father, can we get an even bigger Christmas tree this year?"
I begged.

The ceilings in our apartment were exceptionally high, and
we always got a very tall tree.

"We'll see," Father said. "It's not Christmas Eve yet, so you
know you'll have to wait."

I was looking forward to bringing a fresh tree indoors to
decorate with small apples and packets of *gotina*, the sugary
sweet caramels made from butter, sugar, and cream, wrapped in
colorful, shiny paper.

When Christmas Eve finally arrived, we decorated the
tree while waiting for our grandparents to come over for our
holiday dinner. There was a knock at the door and Elga, and
I rushed to open it. Oma and Opa stomped their feet and
brushed the light dusting of snow off their coats and boots in
the hallway before entering.

"Oma and Opa! You're here! Come, look at how we've
decorated the tree!" I exclaimed.

"Let me go to the kitchen first to put down all this food,"
Oma insisted, lugging several large baskets inside.

"Let us help, Oma! Did you bring the *piragi*?" Elga asked as
we each took a basket and followed her to the kitchen.

"Of course I did girls!" She smiled, giving us a big hug.
What would be a Latvian holiday without them?"

Oma's *piragi* were one of our favorite treats, and we had
helped make them just a few days earlier. Oma rolled bread dough
on a floured kitchen table and pressed circles from the dough with
a glass. Elga and I placed a teaspoon of diced and fried bacon and
onion toward the center of the circle. Folding it over to form a
small crescent, we pinched the edges shut before baking.

Elga and I searched through the baskets to find them, and

when we did, we each grabbed one and devoured it. We were sure they tasted better because we had helped.

"Oh, Biruta, look! Oma made *piperkukas*," Elga exclaimed, unwrapping a plate, "and they're still warm!"

Oma had used layers of cloth napkins to cover each plate to keep them warm. The thin gingerbread cookies were in holiday shapes of Christmas trees, wreaths and bells decorated with almonds.

When we reached for one, Oma patted our hands away and then smiled, "Go ahead, but only one. I don't want you to ruin your Christmas dinner."

Elga and I each took a cookie savoring every bite as it melted in our mouths.

Then Oma playfully wrapped an arm around each of us to guide us out of the kitchen.

"Come, girls, let's go read the Christmas story while Mother is putting the finishing touches on our Christmas dinner."

She chased us into the bedroom, and we settled onto the bed. From our frosted windows we saw snowflakes drifting down, covering the ground in a soft blanket of white. It heightened the mood of the holiday. The three of us snuggled together in the warmth of the room, and Oma's gentle voice began reading the familiar Christmas Bible story.

Moments later, I heard noises coming from the other room, "Shhh, Elga, I think I hear Father Christmas."

"Are you sure? I didn't hear anything..." Oma teased.

"I think Biruta's right. We should check," Elga said as we wiggled out of Oma's embrace.

Running into the darkened living room, we were met by a soft radiance emanating from one corner of the room. Each branch of the Christmas tree was shimmering with small wax candles accenting the decorations we had put on earlier in the day. When the hot candle wax dripped onto the branches, it smoldered on the freshly cut tree giving off a wonderful piney scent. The smell of the tree, along with the delicious aromas of our holiday dinner, swirled in the air. It could only mean it was Christmas.

We turned to see Father and Mother, Oma and Opa standing with their arms around each other, beaming at us.

"Is everyone ready for dinner?" Mother asked.

"Yes!" everyone chorused.

Elga and I turned to see the dining room table and gasped. "Mother, it's beautiful!"

Mother's best china sat at each place setting with white candlesticks glowing in the center of the table. The candles glistened on the golden roast goose stuffed with apples and raisins. Separate bowls held generous portions of sauerkraut and potato dumplings. My mouth watered at the delicious smells.

Elga and I took our seats and wolfed down our food while the rest of the family lingered over the Christmas Eve dinner. Afterward, the family gathered around Mother to sing Christmas carols while she played the piano. It was hard being patient, as Elga and I had seen the unwrapped toys and dolls waiting for us under the tree.

After the carols, Mother yawned and looked at Father, Oma, and Opa.

"I'm tired. Maybe we should wait for gifts until tomorrow morning?"

"No!" Elga and I cried out, but I had seen her wink at Father.

"Alright, you two have been very patient," Mother said, smiling at us as we dashed toward the tree.

Over the coming years, I'd often revisit my holiday memories of Christmas and longed to experience the serenity and security of my former life. I didn't realize this would be the last Christmas Father, Mother, Elga, and I would have at Alexander Heights in the only home I had ever known.

My childhood in Riga with my family was as close to being charmed as I would ever remember. I would dream of playing on the grounds of Alexander Heights and my summers with Oma and Opa at their Mezparks home. I'd cherish the days of splashing on the shores of Lake Kisezers, going to the zoo, and the sweet sounds of music emanating from their home.

On that late summer night in Mezparks, the adult conversation I had overheard and didn't understand was regarding the Russian and German non-aggression treaty of August 1939, the Molotov-Ribbentrop Pact. That summer, the adults worried about what impact it would have on Latvia and the Baltic states.

If I could have taken any meaning from those discussions, I might have been better prepared. However, at the tender age of nine, I didn't understand the world much beyond the circle of my family. Even the adults couldn't have anticipated the onslaught of change that was to come. These idyllic chapters of my family life were about to come to an end and nothing would ever be the same.

CHAPTER 3
Adaptations

World War II began on September 1, 1939, when the Germans invaded Poland. Britain and France, in defense of its ally, declared war on Germany. In keeping with its non-aggression agreement, Russia took no action against them. The independent Baltic countries of Latvia, Lithuania, and Estonia took positions of neutrality.

The Molotov-Ribbentrop pact between Germany and Russia also included a secret clause that was not disclosed until the end of World War II. It divided Eastern Europe between the two powers assigning Latvia and the other Baltic countries to the Soviets.

When Nazi forces, in violation of their pact, continued to take over large parts of Eastern Europe and invaded France, the Soviets became concerned. Stalin coerced the Baltic countries, under threat of invasion, to sign a mutual assistance agreement. It gave the Soviets the right to establish military bases within the Baltic borders. By October 1939, 30,000 Russian troops were stationed in Latvia, 25,000 in Estonia, and 20,000 in Lithuania.[2]

I n January of 1940, Elga and I turned 10 years old. The war in Europe had been going on for a little over four months. Russian troops had arrived in Latvia, but nothing in my daily life had changed. I went to school, came home, and did my homework and chores.

Our family routines remained the same as well. When Father and Mother returned from work, we ate dinner as a family. After we had eaten, Elga and I sat quietly in our chairs while Father and Mother discussed work, local news, and then asked us a few questions about our day. In the evening, as we had always done, the four of us retired to the living room. We spent time together listening to music on the radio, playing games, or reading before Elga and I went to bed.

The presence of Soviet troops in Riga was only noticed when, on occasion, we saw them in small groups in the central city or riding on the streetcar. Behind their backs, Elga and I laughed about the Russian uniforms with their funny-looking hats. The caps, called *budenovkas*, came to a point on top of their heads. To me, they resembled the pictures I had seen of the onioned domes of Red Square in Moscow. Elga and I giggled each time we saw them.

I certainly knew about the war in Europe, but it meant little to me, and I paid little attention to it. Our pleasant family evenings were only interrupted by random radio news bulletins about conflicts on other parts of the continent. Sometimes Father and Mother stopped what they were doing to listen to the reports. Since the Baltic states had declared neutrality, they didn't seem alarmed. I felt safe in the warmth of our home and our daily routines.

In mid-June each year, our parents planned a week-long family vacation in Jurmala. It was a seaside resort on the Baltic

Sea about 20 miles outside of Riga. At the breakfast table the morning before our planned trip, Father snapped the newspaper open to the front page, and upon reading it, scowled.

"Look at this," he said, addressing Mother. "Russia is accusing the Baltic states of defying their mutual assistance treaty."

"That's laughable," Mother said, pouring herself some coffee. "How can they make that accusation? The Russian troops stationed here far outnumber all the Baltic troops combined. They're just making excuses to keep their soldiers here."

"It gets even worse. Listen to this," Father said, briskly rustling the pages. "There's been a Soviet skirmish at a Latvian border post. Some Latvian soldiers, as well as civilians, have been killed."

"Oh, no!" Mother gasped. She stood up and went over to stand behind Father, looking over his shoulder to see the article. "What about our vacation? Is it sensible for us to leave now?"

"What?" Elga cried out.

"Does that mean we can't go to the seashore?" I asked.

"No, girls," Father declared, setting the paper down. He took a deep breath and turned to Mother.

"Elsa, the assault is nowhere near us, and there's nothing we can do about it."

He paused and added in a softer tone, trying to reassure her.

"The Russian troops have been here for months building up their war defenses and until now, without incident. We've earned this vacation, and we need the time away. We'll go as we planned. We may not have another opportunity."

Mother sighed, "I guess you're right. We probably need a distraction from all this war news. Anyway, we won't be far from home."

With Mother's concerns pacified, we took a train to Jurmala the next morning.

The next several days, our family enjoyed the beach relaxing in the sun, walking along the shore, and swimming in the Baltic Sea. Toward the end of the week, Father and Mother learned from newly arriving vacationers that Russian tanks had rolled into Riga. Concerns escalated. Clusters of Latvians gathered on the beaches and in the local cafes to ask what anyone had heard. No one seemed to know.

Our family was just a few miles from Riga but cut off from the events in the city. Father picked up a newspaper at a local shop, scanned the front pages, and then flipped through the rest, finding nothing about the Soviets.

"Paris fell to the Nazis three days ago, so the paper is full of articles about the collapse of France. There are no reports of any Russian operations in the Baltics," he said with a huff.

Lacking further news, Father and Mother were anxious to return home. They hired a car to take us back to Alexander Heights the next day.

In the morning, the car took our family on a route through downtown Riga. Not knowing what to expect, Elga and I were shocked at what we saw. We pressed our noses to the car's cool glass windows. We had seen random groups of soldiers before, but now it appeared as if the whole Russian army was in the city. Huge military tanks sat at major intersections, and smaller armored vehicles buzzed through the streets. Even more alarming was that the soldiers were armed.

"Biruta, look!" Elga cried. "They have bullets strapped across their chests!"

"And rifles on their backs!" I shuddered.

As the car slowed to pass through a checkpoint, a Russian soldier scowled through the front windshield. I slid down on the car seat, trying to avoid his gaze.

"Why are they stopping us? Are they going to arrest us?"

"Shhhh," Mother said, putting an arm around my shoulder. "No, Biruta, he's just checking our identification papers."

Father cranked open a window and handed him our papers. We sat in silence as the soldier studied and returned them. He waved us through, and Father closed the window.

"We'll be home in a few minutes, and we'll talk then," Mother said, staring ahead.

I was gripped with fear and my breath quickened. When the car finally drove through the familiar gates of Alexander Heights, I breathed a sigh of relief.

We unloaded our luggage and entered the apartment. Mother set down her bags in the living room and turned towards Father. Despite several days in the sun, her face was drained of color. She spoke in hushed tones as if she were afraid someone might be listening.

"Hermanis, what does all of this mean?"

"I'm not sure," Father said, rubbing the back of his neck. "Obviously, more of the Russian army has come to Riga. Let's hope they're just shoring up their war defenses. We need to take this one day at a time and see what develops."

Over the next several days, my parents learned little. With rumor and innuendo flying in the city, there was an uneasy tension in the air. Until the situation became more apparent, Elga and I stayed with our parents at Alexander Heights instead of going to Oma's and Opa's for the summer.

One evening after Elga and I had gone to bed, we lay awake, as we typically did, whispering to each other in the dark. Father and Mother were in the living room, listening to the news on the radio turned down low.

Suddenly, Father's raised voice broke the stillness.

"Elsa, did you hear that? The Soviets are requiring new elections in the Baltics and proposing their own slate of communist candidates! This can only be bad news!"

Elga and I weren't accustomed to the tone in Father's voice, and it frightened us. We slipped out of bed and tiptoed to the door of our room, cracking it open to hear better.

"Shhh, Hermanis, the girls…," Mother said, lowering her voice. "A communist takeover would never happen. Latvians are still the majority in the country and would never allow it."

"I'm not so certain," Father said. "With the war, more and more Russians are arriving every day. The situation is tenuous."

"Well," Mother sighed, "there's nothing we can do about it. I'm tired and going to bed."

Elga and I heard her get up and cross the room. A few minutes later, Father snapped off the radio. He pushed back his chair, scraping it against the floor, and clicked off the lights to follow her. He sharply closed their bedroom door behind him.

In their room, their conversation continued. Elga and I strained to hear what was being said, but we only heard muffled voices before it became silent.

"I think they've gone to bed," I whispered to Elga. "But what's a communist, and why is Father so upset?"

"I don't know," she whispered back. "It sounds like Father is afraid about some kind of election."

Holding hands, we padded back to our beds and pulled up our covers. I reached for my stuffed animal at the foot of the bed and held onto it tightly before falling asleep. Later, I woke up in a cold sweat dreaming about armed Russian soldiers in their funny pointed caps poking their rifles at Father.

The following night, Elga and I became even more concerned. The typical family after-dinner conversation was cut short. Father and Mother excused themselves from the table, and we didn't go into the living room like we usually did.

"I'm sorry, girls. Why don't you read to yourselves in your room tonight or play a game?" Mother instructed, giving us both a hug. "Father and I need to talk."

Using hushed tones, they walked to their bedroom and closed the door. As they left, we overheard Father cautioning Mother.

"We must be careful about what we say outside the apartment, especially here at work. Some people support the communist party and may report us to the authorities."

I froze for a moment and then spoke to Elga.

"I don't understand. What authorities are they talking about, and why would they report Father and Mother? They've never done anything wrong."

"I don't know," Elga said, "but I'm sure it has something to do with the Russians."

❧

It was mid-July 1940. A month had passed since additional Soviet troops had entered Riga, and new elections were scheduled. On the morning the polls opened, we heard a loud pounding on the door, waking the household.

"Hello! Hermanis, Elsa! Are you up? Let me in!"

Elga and I rubbed the sleep from our eyes and got up to listen from our bedroom door. We recognized the voice. It was

Father's younger brother, our uncle Oskars, who had come to our apartment.

"Good, both of you are here. I've just come from voting," he said, leaning on the door frame to catch his breath. "Russian officials are monitoring the elections! There are two ballot boxes. One for the communist slate and one for the non-communists. They can see in which box people are placing their ballots!"

"What!" Father cried out. "Then, we won't vote!"

"You must," uncle Oskars said. "They are keeping records of who has voted. Now that the turnout is low, they are deploying soldiers to bring people to the polls. No one dares refuse to cast a ballot, or they'll be thrown in jail."

Father groaned, "If the communist party is voted in, Latvia's independence is over."

"Hermanis, this is much worse than we expected," Mother responded, her voice shaking. "We have to go to the polls. We can't put our family in danger by not voting."

Elga and I looked at each other and ran to Father and Mother.

"What's happening?" we cried.

Father looked at uncle Oskars and then at us. "It's alright, girls. I know this is a lot of excitement for one morning. We've just gotten some unexpected news about the elections. It shouldn't concern you."

Mother tousled our hair and gave us our morning hug.

"Go on, girls. Go to the kitchen and get some breakfast from Christina. Father and I will need to vote this morning. We'll be back soon. It will be fine."

They left with uncle Oskars, and Elga and I hurried to the kitchen.

"Christina, do you think Father and Mother will be alright?" I asked.

"Yes, I'm sure they will be," Christina said with an uneasy smile, but Elga and I noticed her hands trembling as she served us our breakfast. We wolfed down our oatmeal porridge and ran to the window to wait for our parents' return.

The minutes ticked by. An hour later, we saw Father and Mother coming up the walk, their faces grim. They entered the apartment, and we rushed down the hallway only to stop in our tracks.

Father was talking to Christina.

"You must go to vote, too," he said. "Those who don't are being taken into custody. I've seen what's done in the prisons to those who don't follow their orders."

Frightened, Elga and I and ran to our parents. Father turned sharply away from Christina, and clenched his jaw, seeing that we might have overheard. Mother stooped to open her arms wide to us, and we fell into them, shouting, "Is everything okay?"

"Of course, girls. We just needed to vote," Mother reassured us, casting a fleeting glance up at Father.

Days later, Elga and I overheard our parents talking about the results. It appeared the majority of the ballots cast in Latvia overwhelming sanctioned the new Soviet Communist government. It was the same for the elections in both Lithuania and Estonia.

"What do you think this will mean for the Baltics?" Mother asked Father.

"I don't know," he responded. "Whatever it is, judging by the number of soldiers stationed here, they'll carry their authority out by force."

Our everyday lives resumed, and Father and Mother continued to work at the hospital. Father arrived home late on the days he consulted at the prison. Shortly after the election; however, he was back earlier than expected. Pausing in the foyer before entering the room, Father straightened his shoulders, walked straight past Elga and me, and went over to embrace Mother. After a few moments, he pulled away from her and gazed into her eyes.

"Elsa," he said, his voice heavy, "The Soviets have taken over the prisons. They've released me from my consulting job and replaced all Latvian employees with their own."

He paused, massaging his temple and continued, "The Russians are jailing dozens of Latvians on trumped-up charges. I'm sure they assume we'd be sympathetic to our fellow citizens and have replaced us with their own."

"Oh, Hermanis," Mother said, pulling him back into her arms. "We can manage without the extra income, but jailing Latvians for no reason is unthinkable!"

Together they walked away arm-in-arm commiserating on what had just happened. With no explanation, Elga and I were left to wonder on our own.

I stared at Elga, "Do you think Father is in danger?"

"I don't think so," Elga replied. "But I don't know why he can't work at the prison anymore."

In the following days, Elga and I became even more concerned. The typical light-hearted dinner banter was cut short. Father and Mother grimaced when they listened to the news. Instead of our family evenings together, our parents retired to their room to talk, and Elga and I were expected to entertain ourselves alone.

I sighed and flipped open one of my books. "Elga, why do you think Father and Mother aren't talking to us anymore?"

Scowling back at me, Elga replied, "I don't know." She snapped her book shut and said, "I wish they'd tell us what's going on."

❧

The next night after dinner, Elga and I were surprised when Father and Mother asked us to join them in the living room.

"Come, girls, sit down beside me," Mother said, guiding us onto the sofa next to her. Father sat across from us in his customary chair. "We need to talk about what's happening."

Elga and I glanced at each other, flashing knowing smiles. They disappeared when we saw the stern expressions on our parents' faces. I looked down at my feet, swinging them back and forth as I sat on the sofa.

Mother put a hand on my legs to still me as she spoke. Taking a deep breath, Mother glanced over at Father before she began.

"You know that a few days ago, the Russians took over the prison where Father was working. Well, they've taken over the hospital as well. All the psychiatrists have been let go."

Taking a moment for the information to register with us, she continued. "At least for now, I can continue working at the lab, but since Father is no longer working at the hospital…" she said, clutching her hand to her throat, her eyes glistening, "…we are being told we can no longer live at Alexander Heights."

Elga and I stared at each other with our mouths open. What was she saying?

Finally understanding the implications, Elga jumped to her feet and blurted out, "How can you let them do this to us? Why do we have to leave? This is the only place we have ever lived!"

For a few moments, I sat in silence and held my stomach to stifle a dull ache. Turning to Mother, the words catching in my throat, I choked out, "But where will we live?"

"Yes, where will we live?" Elga echoed, plopping herself back down onto the sofa.

Mother, unable to speak at this point, pulled us in closer. Father came over to kneel before us in front of the couch and took our hands.

Looking at us, he said, "We've talked it over with Oma and Opa. We'll be moving in with them."

Elga and I didn't say anything as we took in what he said.

Elga frowned. "But Oma and Opa's house is so small. We can't all live there."

"The Russians have taken over all private property and established new rules," Father explained. "A certain number of people are required to live in each household depending on its square footage. Random people are being assigned to private homes to meet the occupancy rules."

Elga and I looked at each other with blank stares. Father noticed our confusion and said in a softer tone, "If we move in with Oma and Opa, they won't be required to take in strangers into their home. It will benefit us all."

Not caring to understand the reason, I only heard that we'd be moving in with Oma and Opa. A sense of relief replaced the fear I had felt just minutes earlier. Although our family would have to leave our apartment at Alexander Heights, we would be living in our grandparents' familiar home.

Clearing her throat, Mother explained, "Both of you will have your summer room upstairs, of course. Father and I will use Opa's downstairs office for our bedroom. It will be crowded, but we'll have to make do."

All of a sudden, the world looked a little brighter. Smiling, I locked eyes with Elga, and she smiled back. We stood up and joined hands, dancing around the room, singing out, "Oma and Opa's, Oma and Opa's!" until we fell on the floor laughing.

Mother stood up, hands on her hips looking at us in mock irritation, "I can't believe you girls! One minute you're upset and angry, and the next, you are dancing around the room!"

Shaking her head, she smiled for the first time in days and then became serious. "It will be wonderful to be with Oma and Opa, but there'll be a lot of changes."

❧

The next day, our family prepared to leave Alexander Heights. Elga and I piled our well-worn toys and books in the center of our room, ready to pack them. Mother appeared in the doorway carrying two boxes.

"No, girls, you can't take all of that," she said. "Only one box for each of you and get rid of some of your older toys."

As she walked away, Elga whispered to me, "I don't care what she says, I'm not getting rid of my favorites."

Smiling back, I nodded in agreement.

When we finished packing, Elga and I strayed to the front room to watch some of the family effects being loaded for Mezparks. We stopped in our tracks to see furniture covered in sheets. The sofa where we curled up with Mother in the evenings, Father's overstuffed chair, the dining room set which had hosted so many of our family holiday dinners were all in their familiar places.

Seeing our puzzled expressions, Mother smiled sadly and said, "There simply won't be enough room for everything at Oma and Opa's."

Looking at all that had to be left behind, a lump formed in my throat. Feeling helpless and seeing there was not much else we could do, Elga and I wandered outside.

We strolled over to the familiar chestnut tree next to our bedroom window. Tears welled in the corners of my eyes as I looked up at the tree's leaf-laden branches. It would no longer mark off the seasons for us.

At the base of the tree, a bur had split open. Picking it up, a nut was revealed. I removed it and ran my fingers over its smooth, shiny brown hull. Wanting it as a remembrance, I slipped it into my pocket. I'd store it in my drawstring sachel along with my coins and other small keepsakes to take with me to Mezparks.

Before going back indoors, I scanned the property one last time and said a silent good-bye to what had been my playground. By evicting our family from Alexander Heights, the Russians were taking away more than Father's livelihood and our family home. They were taking away my childhood.

CHAPTER 4

Riga, Latvia | June 1940 - June 1941

"The Year of Terror"

A s expected, Oma and Opa welcomed us into their home with open arms. The small bungalow that had been home to Elga and me during our summers became home for our entire family. Opa's den on the first floor became my parents' bedroom. The massive desk in the room was moved out into the living room for Father's office. Father would supplement the family income by opening a small private practice out of Oma's and Opa's home. The large enclosed veranda where Elga and I used to play became Father's waiting room. It was an adjustment, but over time, our new living situation worked for all of us.

In the fall, Elga and I went back to school. The building and the teachers all looked the same. Over the summer, some students had grown a little taller, but the faces remained familiar. While it appeared that nothing had changed, everything had.

In every classroom where the Latvian president's picture had once hung, authoritarian portraits of Lenin and Stalin replaced them. We no longer learned about Latvian history but studied communist leaders, their doctrine, and their superior form of government. I didn't care about political philosophies and merely accepted it as a part of our new lessons.

Out in the schoolyard during a break, a group of our friends shouted out to Elga and me.

"Hey, look, there are 'the sisters'!"

It was the nickname our friends had given us and made us feel special.

We ran toward them, and they shouted, "Are you coming to The Pioneer Club after school today?"

The purpose of the club was to reinforce the communist principles taught in the classroom. Even though we cherished the time with our friends, the club wasn't all that interesting to us. Elga and I were secretly pleased our parents didn't insist that we go. It also freed us from having to wear the Pioneer uniform of blue skirts or pants, white shirts, and a red neckerchief to school each day.

Our friends told us the club rewarded student loyalty. Children were encouraged to report any adults, including their parents, who were talking against the new regime. Elga and I were relieved not to be put in that position.

"No, we can't go," I said, looking down at the ground. "We need to get home after school."

Trying to sound important, Elga added, "With the war and food shortages, Oma needs our help in her garden."

It was an excuse for us not to attend the after-school meetings, and we were glad to spend the extra time with Oma.

~∾∾

One evening, I struggled with a school assignment and was relieved to have finished it. Eager to show Mother, I ran to her.

"Mother, look what I've written!"

Smiling, Mother put down her book and reached for my paper. As she began reading, her smile faded, and small creases formed in her brow. After a few tense moments, she struggled to find something to say.

She laid the paper down and said in an even tone, "My Biruta, this certainly shows what they're teaching you in school these days."

Mother's less than enthusiastic response crushed me. It was not what I had expected. She had seen how hard I'd been working and usually acknowledged my efforts. Unsure that I had done well, I was reluctant to hand in my paper at school the next day.

A few days later, the teacher handed back my graded assignment. She complimented my poem praising Stalin to the entire class. I was confused by my teacher's flattery. When I saw Mother at home, I said nothing. I couldn't bear to ask her why she hadn't liked my poem.

Years later, I realized it was the subject of the poem, and not me that Mother couldn't compliment. She was shocked at what I was being taught at school. If the school personnel had any indication of anti-communist sentiments coming from my home, they would have reported my parents to the new government authorities. They would've been questioned or maybe even jailed.

Mother, Father, Oma, and Opa were careful about the subjects being discussed when Elga and I were present. They shielded us from the news of war and the Soviets in Latvia. For all their caution, they didn't realize how easy it was for Elga and me to eavesdrop from our bedroom upstairs.

One Sunday afternoon, Elga and I were in our room when friends of my parents dropped in for a visit. There was light chatter coming from the living room as everyone settled in.

"Elsa, Hermanis, have you heard?" the husband asked my parents.

As if on cue, Elga's and my ears perked up. We crept to the top of the stairs to listen.

"Rumors are that Russian soldiers have been committing atrocities in the countryside."

"Yes," his wife said, "we're fortunate to live in the city where there are many more people..."

The husband, anxious to share his news, interrupted his wife, "They say those who oppose the Russians are being tortured in the prisons... or even shot."

I squeezed my eyes shut and covered my ears with my hands. I couldn't believe what I was hearing, but I wanted to know more. Uncovering my ears, I continued to listen.

"Do you think it is true?" Mother asked.

"Unfortunately, yes," Father replied. "From what I've seen in the prisons, I wouldn't doubt people are being tortured or killed."

Eyes wide open, Elga and I gawked at each other. Father was confirming it!

"It's even worse," the wife continued. "They say soldiers in the countryside are abusing women and children." Her dramatic pause allowed for her words to take effect, and then she said, "I'd never allow it. If any Russian tried to touch my daughter or me, I'd kill ourselves first."

Hearing about the atrocities and what the mother was willing to do made me swoon. Elga grabbed me to steady me. Horrified, I had heard enough. I grabbed Elga's hand and pulled her back into our room. For a while, we didn't speak. Then in a whisper, we promised each other not to tell anyone that we'd been listening or what we had heard.

That night, I awoke screaming and sobbing from unspeakable nightmares. Mother and Oma rushed into our bedroom. Mother sat on my bed, rocking me in her arms, while Oma sang lullabies, and Elga looked on in stunned silence.

"Heavens, Biruta," Oma said, stroking my damp forehead. "What thoughts could have frightened you so?"

Glancing at Elga and remembering our promise, she didn't say a word. Mother held me until my tears subsided, and eventually, I fell into a fitful sleep.

෴

A few nights later, Opa returned from work to tell the family about an incident he witnessed in the city.

"I saw a Russian soldier stopping a local man to ask for directions. The man shrugged his shoulders, pretending not to understand and pointed the soldier toward Moscow. As the soldier walked away," Opa said with a sly grin, "'the man muttered under his breath. 'All of you need to go back to Moscow'."

"Oh, my," Oma said. "It's what everyone is thinking. The Russians are a constant reminder that our freedom has been lost."

"Yes, but it's worse than that," Opa said, his voice rising. "No one feels safe anymore. We are being watched, and we have to watch what we say. We can't have any social gatherings for fear of being labeled anti-communist. The Soviets consider our former lives 'bourgeois'. Evidence is everywhere their socialist society is replacing ours. Anyone who thinks differently simply disappears."

"Hush," Oma said, dramatically. "You don't want anyone else to hear."

⤳

On the morning of June 14th, 1941, the early days of summer called to Elga and me. We woke up at first light.

"Biruta, do you think Oma will let us ride our bikes around the neighborhood?" Elga exclaimed.

"I don't see why not," I said, mirroring Elga's enthusiasm.

We skipped down the stairs to ask Oma.

"That's fine, girls," she said, "but only around the block. I want you to stay nearby."

"Thanks, Oma," I yelled. We raced out the door, grabbed our bikes, and took off.

As we turned the corner, we noticed an army truck in front of a neighbor's house. With caution we pedaled closer and saw Russian soldiers escorting a family out of their home.

The man, who we knew to be the father, was shouting, "You can't do this! We've done nothing wrong!" as a soldier nudged him along with the butt of his rifle.

Elga and I slammed on our brakes, the wheels crunching to a halt on the pavement. We jumped off our bikes, watching in alarm from a distance as the spectacle unfolded.

Armed soldiers ignored the father's pleas and continued pushing him forward. The mother, her skirt and blouse askew as if she had pulled them on in a hurry, was crying. The boy, who Elga and I recognized from school, clung to his mother sobbing. Forcibly, the family was shoved to the back of the truck. Then we noticed other families standing shoulder-to-shoulder like herded animals in the three-sided truck bed. Frightened, Elga and I spun our bikes around and pedaled home as fast as we could. Dropping our bikes at the front door, we ran into the kitchen, out of breath.

"Oma! Something horrible is happening!" Elga cried. "Russian soldiers are taking families away in trucks!"

"Heavens!" Oma exclaimed, wiping her hands on her apron.

"Will they come for us, too?" I gasped in horror.

"Hermanis, Opa!" Oma called out. "Something is going on down the street! Where is Elsa?"

"She went into work at the hospital early this morning," Father replied as he and Opa entered the kitchen. "What's all the commotion?"

"The girls have just seen Russian soldiers taking away neighboring families in trucks," Oma said, encircling her arms around us as we trembled.

"What! In Mezparks?" Father bellowed.

He strode across the room and knelt before us. Elga and I flew into his arms. He held us until we calmed, and then he placed us at arm's length.

"Tell me, girls, what did you see?" he asked in a soothing but persistent tone.

With our grandparents listening, we told him everything we had seen.

Father pulled us back into his arms. "I'm sure there's an explanation. You needn't worry, girls. No one is coming after us."

Oma looked at Father aghast, "But in the prisons, I thought you saw..."

"I haven't worked in the prison for over a year," Father said, cutting Oma off with a penetrating look. "The girls have been frightened enough for one day. We needn't scare them more."

"I'm sorry," Oma said, looking down, regretting she had spoken. "Your Father's right, dears. There's no reason to be afraid," she said as she planted a kiss on the top of our heads.

Elga and I shadowed Oma for the rest of the day. Anytime a door opened or closed, we jumped. We worried that at any moment, Russian soldiers might barge into our home and take us. Mother returned from work later that afternoon, and Elga and I rushed into her arms the minute she stepped in the door.

"My, what's the occasion for such a greeting?" Mother asked.

Father, Oma, and Opa joined us in the front room, and she was informed about what had transpired that morning.

"What an awful thing to have witnessed!" Mother said, embracing us. "But it's over, and we're all safe."

At the same time, I couldn't ignore the look she gave Father. I shuddered to think she knew more than she was telling us. Mother held Elga and me several minutes longer, reassuring us. Then she took a deep breath and released us.

"Girls, I need to talk to your father. Would you mind terribly if I ask you to go upstairs to your room for a bit?"

Heaving heavy sighs, Elga and I obeyed Mother and trudged up the stairs. However, instead of going to our room, we took our station at the top of the stairs.

We fell silent, and Mother began speaking to Father in low tones, "My Russian supervisor was surprised to see me at work this morning."

"Whatever do you mean?" Father said in alarm.

Mother's voice was shaky, "He confided to me that our family had been on the deportation list. When the soldiers didn't find us at Alexander Heights, they went elsewhere."

She paused to clear her throat, "The supervisor said the raids are over now, but they'll be looking for us the next time they come. We can only pray it won't be anytime soon."

Father groaned. Elga and I looked at each other, eyes bulging and covering our mouths. It had only been by chance that our family wasn't on one of those trucks. Had the soldiers known where we were living, our family would have been taken away too.

Elga and I hardly had time to process the information before we heard Father and Mother's footsteps moving toward the stairs. We scampered back into our room, grabbing books and falling on our beds, pretending to read. Father and Mother entered, and one sat next to each of us on our beds.

"You must both be badly shaken by what you saw this morning," Mother said. "We wanted to make sure you were alright."

"Yes," Father said. "I'm sorry you had to see it. It must have been very frightening."

Elga and I nodded, snuggling closer to them.

"It was horrible. I've never been so scared," Elga said, her voice quivering.

Chills ran up and down my spine, recalling the scene of our classmate's family being taken away at gunpoint and our parents' overheard conversation.

I whimpered and asked Mother, "It's all over, right?"

"Yes, I've been told the raids are over, and our family

is safe," Mother said. She looked at each of us, avoiding Father's gaze and gave each an extra hug.

"Remember, we'll always be there for you and will always protect you," Father said. He stood up and leaned over to kiss us each on the cheek.

"Are you girls settled enough to come down for some of Oma's dinner?' Mother asked.

"Yes!" Elga and I chorused, and we followed Father and Mother down the stairs.

CHAPTER 5
Riga | June 1941 - Fall 1943, Liberators

The evening of June 13th, 1941, into the morning of the 14th, was later called the "Night of Terror" in Latvia. Soviet troops rousted over 15,000 Latvians from their beds, arresting them for alleged anti-communist activities. Families were torn apart as husbands were separated from their wives and children, and were herded like cattle onto railroad boxcars to be shipped to slave labor camps in Siberia.

Those who were seized traveled thousands of miles across Russia in overcrowded train cars with little food and poor sanitation. Many died. When the survivors reached Siberia, they were exposed to frigid temperatures and starvation in the harsh conditions of the work camps. Many more perished.

Similar raids were conducted in Lithuania and Estonia. In the first year of Soviet occupation, from June 1940 to June 1941, the number confirmed executed, conscripted, or deported is estimated at a minimum of 124,467.[3] The Western world, not knowing the extent of Stalin's barbarity, did not directly interfere with their Soviet ally in the war.

Ten days after the Soviet raids, welcomed news came to the Baltics on June 23, 1941.

"Elsa, Hermanis, have you heard?" Opa asked Father and Mother as he returned from work. "German troops are entering Latvia, and the Soviets are retreating!"

"What good news!" Oma exclaimed. "If the Russians leave, perhaps our independence will be restored."

"I wouldn't go that far," Father said. "There's a war going on. We've seen Stalin's barbarity, but we don't know anything about Hitler."

"Well, at least we won't have to look around every corner in fear of being reported to the Communist authorities," Mother asserted.

"Or of being rounded up in the middle of the night," Opa added.

"Praise the Lord for that!" Oma said.

"Biruta, Elga come look," Opa said as he walked over to the living room window and held the curtain back. "You can actually see signs of the Russian retreat. See those long, low patches of gray on the horizon? They're clouds of dust created by Russian tanks and trucks leaving the city."

Pleased with the news and evidence of the Soviet departure, our family sat down for our quiet evening dinner. No sooner had we begun to eat when a massive explosion rocked the foundation. Elga and I shrieked and clung to the table. Some serving dishes Oma had placed on the sideboard clattered to the floor, adding to the clamor.

"Good heavens! What was that!" Oma shouted as she and Mother ran over to keep the rest of the dishware from falling.

Opa went back to the living room window to look outside.

"Smoke is coming from the armory nearby. The Soviets must

be destroying their arsenal to keep it from falling into the hands of the Germans."

Scowling, Father stated, "Let's hope they can keep their detonations under better control."

"Good riddance to the Soviets," Oma huffed, taking the dishes to the kitchen. "I only wish they'd leave with a little less fanfare."

Though not as intense, random blasts from the armory continued throughout the evening. The sounds only intensified as they echoed off the houses in Mezparks, disturbing the peaceful neighborhood. When it was time for Elga and me to turn in for the night, we went to our beds and pulled the covers over our heads.

"Psst, Biruta, are you awake?" Elga whispered.

"Are you crazy? How can anyone sleep through this?" I said. "I'm scared. Let's go downstairs and sleep on the living room sofa closer to Father and Mother."

In the dark, we grabbed our pillows and blankets, stole down the stairs, and crawled onto the sofa. Resting on the lumpy cushions, we held on to each other, trying to fall asleep. Just as I was drifting off, the loudest explosion yet shook the house to its core. Rugs seemed to jump off the floor, and a loud crash of breaking glass came from the veranda. Elga and I screamed and ran into our parents' bedroom, jumping onto their bed.

"Are we being bombed?!" we cried as Mother cradled us.

"No," Father said with reassurance as Oma and Opa joined us in the room. "It's as Opa suspected. The Russians are leaving nothing in their armory behind."

Trembling with fright, I stilled my breath, waiting for the next explosion. I heard only the sound of the ticking clock in our parents' bedroom. For half an hour, we heard nothing more.

"I think it's over and safe to go back to bed," Opa declared. "We'll have to wait until morning to check the damage."

He and Oma went upstairs, but Elga and I stayed with Father and Mother. When our eyelids fluttered, and we couldn't stay awake any longer, Mother gently shook us.

"Girls, I think we'll all sleep better in our own beds. How about going back to your room?"

Grumbling and staggering out of our parents' bedroom, Elga and I didn't go upstairs but went straight to the living room sofa. Exhausted from the long night, we fell onto our pillows, pulled up our blankets, and drifted off to sleep.

Early the next morning, Oma and Opa came downstairs, anxious to inspect the destruction from last evening. Elga and I got up from the sofa, stretched, and rubbed the sleep from our eyes. We each grabbed a corner of Oma's nightgown and followed our grandparents across the room.

Opa went to the door of the large veranda where the windows faced the ammunition depot. Trying to open it, he met resistance. Shoving at the door with his shoulder, it finally gave way. Elga and I looked past our grandparents into the outer room and gasped.

The veranda had absorbed the worst of the blasts, and the windows had been completely blown out. The entire room was a pile of rubble with shards of broken glass and debris littering the floor. Oma and Opa groaned, complaining about the time and cost it would take to repair the damage. Then our eyes drifted to one corner of the room. Amidst the wreckage, a metal object, the size and shape of a large milk bottle, rested on its side next to the outer wall of the living room.

"What in the world is that?" I asked.

"Don't move," Opa said, holding up his arm, blocking us from going any further. "It's an unexploded shell. The force of the blast must have blown it from the armory without it exploding."

We all stood frozen in place, and for a long moment, no one said a word. The shell was directly on the other side of the wall where Elga and I had slept the previous night.

※

By July 7, 1941, just a few weeks later, all of Latvia was under German control. Nazi troops had replaced the retreating Soviets.

One morning, a German officer was in the neighborhood inquiring about temporary housing for himself and three of his fellow soldiers. He came to our house in Mezparks, knocking on Oma and Opa's door. Oma greeted the officer in German, a smile spreading across her face. She had not spoken any German during the Russian occupation for fear of being called out as an enemy sympathizer. Wiping her hand on her apron, she extended it to welcome the officer.

Oma spoke with Opa, reporting the officer's request for lodging. She convinced Opa to allow the soldiers to shelter on the veranda. A bomb squad had disposed of the unexploded shell, and the debris cleared away, but the windows had not been replaced. It made no difference to the officer and his war-weary soldiers. They were only happy to have a roof over their heads.

"Now that we have new guests," Oma said to Elga and me, "you'll have to brush up on your German if you wish to speak to them."

With gestures and our limited German, Elga and I communicated awkwardly with the soldiers. We learned the three youngest were only 18 and 19 years old. Leaving their homes at such a young age must have been difficult for them, and our family made every effort to make them feel welcome.

During the day, the soldiers left the house to drill or attend to their military duties. In the evening after dinner, Oma invited them into the living room to spend time with our family. It appeared the three young soldiers were well educated and had come from good families. Each showed an exceptional talent in one of the fine arts.

Elga and I took a particular liking to the youngest of the three, Walter. He was good looking with blonde hair, blue eyes, and strong chiseled features. He played the piano beautifully. Opa was amazed at his talent at the keyboard. Another one of the soldiers liked to write and recite his own poetry. The third enjoyed creating sketches for all of us.

During the "Horrible Year" of Soviet occupation, people were afraid to gather for "elitist" cultural activities. The music, poems, and sketches of these gifted young soldiers brought back memories of happier times in Mezparks. It reminded me of the carefree summer evening get-togethers with Opa's talented friends before the war had begun.

Elga and I were comfortable in the presence of the three younger soldiers. However, Officer Decker, who had made the initial contact with Oma, was more standoffish. We guessed him to be in his mid-twenties and very much in charge. He took his military duties seriously and carried himself with an arrogant air of authority. Our family called him "Herr Officer" when the soldiers weren't around.

One day returning from a friend's home, Elga and I spotted

"Herr Officer", exiting a streetcar nearby. He was attempting to flirt with some pretty young Latvian girls who had gotten off at the same stop. Officer Decker was behaving in a manner unlike what we had seen at our home. He whistled and hooted, making inappropriate gestures and comments to the girls. Making quite a fool of himself, the girls simply walked away and ignored him.

"He must think he's some kind of ladies' man," Elga giggled, rolling her eyes.

"Lucky for us, we're not old enough for him to show us that kind of attention!" I said as we laughed the rest of the way home.

⚓

As the war progressed, food became less readily available. It was heavily rationed with surpluses going to the German army. One morning after the soldiers had left for the day, Oma waved the family into the kitchen.

"You can't believe what just happened. 'Herr Officer' brought in four eggs this morning and asked me to prepare them. Where he got four eggs, I can only imagine! Doing as he asked, I fried the eggs. I placed them on four separate plates, one for each of the soldiers, and gave them to him. He slid the eggs onto one plate and gulped them all down for himself!"

"Such brazen selfishness!" Oma said, smirking and shaking her head in disbelief.

A few days later, Officer Decker informed our family that the German army had secured centralized and more permanent housing for the soldiers. They were leaving our home. As I stood in the doorway of the veranda watching the soldiers pack their gear, a wave of sadness overcame me.

At age 11, I struggled to understand why these talented young men had to go to war.

As the soldiers left, our family stood on the steps of the empty veranda, waving good-bye. We had let them into our lives, and they had touched each of us. Their special gifts wouldn't be seen or appreciated on the battlefield. Moreover, it was unlikely our paths would ever cross again.

"It's a shame," Father sighed, shoving his hands into his pockets. "The war will certainly change those fine young lads."

As the soldiers' walked away, we watched their silhouettes fade from view. When we could no longer see them, we turned to go back into the house.

꧁

The following summer of 1942, the war in Europe had been fought around our borders for almost three years. It had been a full year since the Germans had ousted the Russians from the country. Unlike the Soviets, the Germans allowed Latvians to keep their social, cultural, and religious practices along with their national flag and anthem. Overall, the Latvians continued to view the Germans as liberators. Hopes were high that after the war, the country's independence would be restored.

One afternoon, Elga and I heard Mother talking to Father after work.

"Hermanis, the Nazis are moving all the psychiatric patients from Alexander Heights. No one knows where they're being taken."

"I'm not surprised," Father said. "I've heard the Nazis are relocating many Latvian Jews and Gypsies. They're being taken to the area of Riga called Maskavas Forstate. Objections to the practice aren't being tolerated. People are forcibly seized without explanation."

Oma, who was in the room, added, "My Jewish friend is frightened that they will be coming for them too. She's given me her jewelry and lamb's skin coat to safeguard – or keep if she doesn't return. The Nazis are treating some as callously as the Communists."

Elga and I looked at each other in alarm. We didn't know such things were happening.

Years later, we learned that from July 1941 to October 1943, the Nazis had created a ghetto in the Riga suburb of Maskavas Forstate. Even more horrific on November 30th and December 8th, 1941, about 24,000 Latvian Jews from the Riga ghetto were killed in or on their way to the Rumbala forest near Riga.[4] It was called the Rumbala massacre, and a monument still stands there for the Jews who lost their lives.

✥

Late one afternoon, Mother called Elga and me in from the garden where we had been helping Oma. It was unusual for her to seek us out immediately upon her return from work. Bewildered, we left the backyard to enter the house. Mother pulled out chairs from the kitchen table, indicating that we should sit down.

"Girls, what do you think about having a German student live with us for the summer?" Mother asked.

Seeing our surprised faces, Mother was amused.

"I know this is unexpected, but a special situation has arisen."

Mother explained that she was the attending physician

to a woman who had been recently hospitalized. The woman, Marianne Rinne, had come to visit her husband in Riga. He was a German military requisitions officer stationed here. Her son was in the army as well. Shortly after Marianne's arrival, she had a psychiatric crisis, requiring hospitalization. During Mother's rounds at the hospital, she noticed a young girl sitting with Marianne day after day. Curious, Mother asked Marianne about her.

The girl was her daughter, Sulbrit, who they called Sulli and was 12 years old, like us. Being on her summer vacation, she had accompanied her mother to Riga. Since Marianne's hospitalization, Sulli spent her days at her mother's bedside, and her evenings with her father, Officer Rinne. It was not ideal, but the family knew no one else in Latvia, and there was no alternative.

When Mother next saw Sulli, she addressed her in German. Mother explained that her mother was doing better but would need to remain hospitalized a while longer. Upon hearing the news, Sulli's face fell.

"I felt bad for Sulli," Mother said to us, "and thought you girls would be good companions. You also know some German."

"We would love her to stay with us!" Elga exclaimed.

"We could teach her some Latvian, too!" I said, already imagining the good times we would have.

"Since you both agree, I'll talk to Officer Rinne and Marianne tomorrow about Sulli staying with us."

The next day, Elga and I waited for Mother to return from work and greeted her at the door. We wanted to hear what Sulli's parents had said.

"The Rinnes graciously accepted the offer. You should've seen how Sulli's face lit up when I told her about the two of you. She'll be here tomorrow and will stay here for the rest of the summer."

The following day, Elga and I repeatedly ran to the window to watch for Sulli's arrival.

"Girls, going to window every few minutes won't make her suddenly appear," Mother laughed. "They'll be here soon enough."

A few moments later, a military vehicle pulled up to the house. A distinguished-looking officer in a crisp German uniform stepped out of the car.

"That must be Sulli's father, Officer Rinne," I said in awe.

"Look, he's going around to open the door for her," Elga stated, equally impressed.

The car door opened, and Sulli jumped out, her shoulder-length brunette braids bouncing. She took her father's arm as they walked up to the house together. All smiles, Elga and I opened the door to greet them. With a broad grin, Sulli smiled back at us, revealing deep dimples in each cheek.

"You really are twins!" Sulli said in German when she noticed our identical dresses and our dark hair styled in the same way. The three of us giggled.

Politely, she extended her hand to Father, Mother, Oma, and Opa. Her charm and warm handshake put all of us at ease. Sulli's father brought in her suitcase and spoke to Father and Mother about last-minute arrangements. Then he kissed his daughter good-bye and left.

Eager to show Sulli our room, Elga and I grabbed her hands and pulled her up the stairs. She entered our bedroom wide-eyed, taking a slow turn around the room.

"This is wonderful," she said. "I've been staying at the hospital or in a barrack for so long. It's nice to be in a real home." She went to the window, gazing out onto the wooded yard below. "It's beautiful here."

"There's even a zoo down the street," Elga said.

"And a swimming lake, too!" I grinned.

"Really! A zoo and a lake? I know this will be a good summer after all. I love my mother, but I was getting bored sitting by her bedside day-after-day."

Sulli stayed with us while her mother recuperated. Over the following weeks, our attachment grew as we worked together in Oma's garden, visited the zoo, or went swimming at the lake. At night we giggled in bed, teaching each other inappropriate words and slang in each other's language. In no time, the three of us were the best of friends. Life felt normal despite the war around us.

However, there was no escaping the war. One late August afternoon, Elga, Sulli, and I sprawled in the shade of *liela priede*, the big pine tree in the backyard. Opa's excited voice came from an open window. He was listening to the latest reports on the radio of Germany's surge into Russia. He spoke in a rush of words to Oma.

"Listen! The Germans are advancing on Stalingrad! They say if Stalingrad falls, Russia's supply lines will be cut. If the Germans captured the city named after Stalin, it would be a great moral victory. Then Hitler can march straight on to Moscow."

"Let's pray it's true," Oma proclaimed. "Maybe this godforsaken war could then be over."

The three of us sat up. Elga and I noticed the sad and faraway look in Sulli's eyes.

"I wish the war was over," Sulli said in a small voice. "Then my father and brother could come home."

I hadn't thought much about Sulli's father and brother

before this, and her words struck me. Father had always been home, and I couldn't imagine it otherwise. I wanted to make Sulli feel better but didn't know what to say. Elga and I looked at each other and then turned to hug Sulli.

～★

Too soon, a chill in the air announced the arrival of fall. With her mother recovered, Sulli needed to go back to school. Officer Rinne would stay in Riga, fulfilling his military obligations, but Sulli and Marianne had to return to Germany.

On the morning Sulli was to leave, Elga and I had long faces as we watched her gather her things from our room. A moment later, we heard a knock at the front door. Mother opened it to greet the Rinnes. The three of us trudged down the stairs and saw our parents in the living room.

Marianne, taking Mother's hands into hers, said, "We can't thank you and the girls enough for everything you've done for Sulli and me this summer."

In a sincere tone, Officer Rinne added, "If there's anything we can ever do for your family, you must let us know. I'll keep in touch."

With a lump in my throat, I turned to Sulli, "Do you think you'll ever come back to Riga again?"

"I'm not sure," Sulli answered, avoiding my gaze. "I'll be back in school, and I don't think father even knows if he'll be stationed here next summer."

Officer Rinne nodded in agreement.

"Then, we might not ever see you again," Elga said sadly.

"I hope that won't be true," she said. "While my father is here, we can keep in contact through him."

We all smiled weakly and wrapped our arms around each other to say good-bye. Sulli walked with her parents to the waiting car. Once inside, Sulli turned to wave from the rear window, and we waved back. I stood by helpless to keep the vehicle from taking our new friend and her parents away.

Over the past few months, Sulli had become like a sister to us, and our parents had become good friends. We hoped we'd see each other again, but we knew the war would make it difficult, if not impossible.

～

A few days later, Elga and I returned to classes with our friends and became involved in the new school year. As Officer Rinne promised, he kept in touch with our family. He let us know how Marianne and Sulli were doing and passed along our news to them. The school term flew by and in the spring of 1943, Elga and I graduated from primary school. We were 13 and looking forward to attending high school in the fall.

At the beginning of summer, our family received an official-looking letter from the German government. Mother tore the envelope open, reading its contents aloud. It was a notification to all Latvian families with adolescent children. Because of the growing food shortages, all entering high school students were required to contribute to the war effort by working on a farm. Mother dropped the notice letting it flutter to the floor.

"Hermanis, what are we going to do? We can't send the girls out into the country to work on some strange farm!" Mother complained.

I recalled the time when Elga and I had overheard

about the Soviet atrocities in the countryside. I thought about my horrible nightmares and shuddered. The Soviet soldiers were gone, but were the German soldiers any different? I grimaced, remembering "Herr Officer's" slurs to the Latvian girls at the streetcar and understood Mother's concerns.

Father paused for a few moments, kneading his temple.

"I have an idea. Remember? My brother Rudolfs owns the family farm in Vidzeme. He's also a county official. I'm sure he could get the necessary permits for the girls to work for him. I'll contact him straightaway."

Within the week, the necessary permits were secured. There was no easy way to travel between Riga and the farm three hours north. During our time working there, Elga and I wouldn't be able to see our family. It would be our first extended time away from home.

Uncle Rudolfs had never married or had any children. We hadn't visited often, but Elga and I knew Uncle Rudolfs and liked him. Several family friends also lived and worked on the farm. In truth, we looked forward to the new experience and, before long, left for Vidzeme.

For the next two months, Elga and I weeded the gardens, gathered vegetables, and brought feed to the farm animals. We even learned to milk the cows. Having our first real jobs and helping with the war effort made us feel grownup.

Despite the hard work, living in the countryside felt like a holiday to us. We were removed from the food shortages in the city and the constant news about the war. We dearly missed Father, Mother, Oma, and Opa and our carefree summers in Mezparks, but Elga and I had each other and were happy.

At the end of the summer, we had fulfilled our work

requirements. We left the tranquil countryside to once again deal with the realities of war in the city. During our time away, food shortages and rationing had only worsened. Oma, clutching our family's coupons, would stand in long lines for hours at requisition centers for food and our basic necessities.

Even the high school experience Elga and I looked forward to had changed entirely. The German army had taken over schools and hospital buildings for military offices and housing. Instead, small groups of students met in private homes for classes. A local fire hall held larger school functions.

Sometimes during our classes, airplanes hummed overhead. We rushed to the windows to see Russian planes flying over the skies of Riga. Often the sightings were followed by the rat-a-tat of German anti-aircraft artillery and streams of tracers. The artillery missed their mark as the planes flew too high, going to other fronts.

After four years of war in Europe, "normal" ceased to exist. At every turn, war now filled our lives. Even worse, there was every indication that the war was inching closer. Radio news reported Soviet battles on Latvia's eastern borders. Fears of the Baltics being overtaken by the Russians again were rising. An air of nervous tension permeated the city. I wanted to turn back the clock to my former comfortable life and thought the war would never end.

CHAPTER 6

Riga | 1943 - 1944 A Change in Circumstances

The Battle of Stalingrad, which had begun at the end of August 1942, was considered by many historians the turning point of WWII in Europe. The German army had marched and fought over 1,000 miles across Russia to get to Stalingrad and battled there for over five months. It was one of the most massive confrontations of WWII and the bloodiest battle in the history of warfare.

In February 1943, the Axis forces in Stalingrad had exhausted their ammunition and food. The remaining units of the German army surrendered.[5] There were two million military and civilian casualties, including an entire German army of 250,000 soldiers who were wiped out. It was a costly defeat for the Germans, giving the Soviets a significant and decisive victory. In the following months, the Soviet forces slowly drove the Nazi troops back across Europe, pushing them toward Germany, where their initial offensive began.

By December 1943, a Soviet re-occupation weighed heavily on the minds of most Latvians. Despite the undercurrent of unease, each one of our family members continued their daily routines. Elga and I were near the mid-point of our first year in high school. Father saw some private patients and worked for the German Health Department in Riga while Mother remained at the lab at Alexander Heights. Opa continued his job at the bank, and Oma managed the household. Despite my parents' and Opa's employment, salaries were low and inflation high. Many things, once readily available, were now considered luxuries, and money did not go far.

The holidays were upon us, but replicating the Christmases of our past was not possible. There would be no tree with candles and decorations of colorfully wrapped candies. Ham or bacon for Oma's *piragi* was not available. Flour and sugar for gingerbread *piperkukas*, if available, were heavily rationed. Spices, like ginger, had not been on hand for years. Our Christmas Eve dinner was limited to meager portions of potato dumplings. For presents, we each drew the name of one family member to create a homemade gift.

The one fixture of the holidays that remained in Oma and Opa's home was the piano. Before we exchanged gifts, as always, we gathered around it to sing carols. Mother sat down at the piano, but before she began to play, she turned to look at us. With a self-conscious grin, she told us she had an announcement. Elga and I narrowed our eyes and looked at each other. In our tight-knit family, there were few secrets.

Mother cleared her throat. "I didn't want to say anything earlier, but it's time all of you know."

She paused before saying, "I'm expecting a baby in May."

Everyone but Father, who knew in advance, gasped in surprise.

Some time ago, when Elga and I asked and were old enough to understand, Oma had told us we probably wouldn't be having another brother or sister. She explained that Mother had developed life-threatening blood clots in her legs following our birth. Many women died from the complication. It was so serious, Father, Oma, and Opa had discussed how they would raise twin babies without Mother. She was bedridden for over a month. Oma came over daily to Alexander Heights to bandage Mother's legs with warm compresses and care for us. It was a blessing Oma had been there, and Mother recovered.

"Oh a baby!" Oma cried out. "This is unexpected news!" Then she considered Mother's past delivery complications and added, "Will you be safe?"

Mother smiled, speaking with confidence to her mother, "What happened years ago is now easily treated with medication. There is no need to be concerned."

Oma and Opa breathed a sigh of relief and went over to Father and Mother to congratulate them by kissing them both on the cheek.

Mother turned to Elga and me. "Well, girls, what do you think?" she asked.

"A new baby! How exciting!" Elga said, speaking for both of us. We looked at Mother, grinning our approval from ear-to-ear.

"And your friends?" she asked.

We'd be turning 14 in just a few weeks. It was likely we would get some stinging comments from classmates about the age difference between us and a new baby brother or sister.

"Who cares what anyone else thinks," I said. "It's wonderful news!"

"I will need to return to work as soon as I'm able after

the delivery," Mother added. "I know you girls have a lot of homework, but Oma will need your help after school."

"Of course!" Elga said.

I enthusiastically agreed, "We'll help in any way we can."

Mother looked at us and smiled, "I knew I could count on both of you."

She turned around, placing her hands on the piano keys and struck up the first chords of "Silent Night". We circled closer to Mother to sing and celebrate the announcement of a new birth.

⌣⋆⋆⋆

Just as good news came unexpectedly to our home at Christmas, one February evening, tragedy struck. Elga and I were in the kitchen, helping Oma prepare dinner. Father and Mother, who had just returned from work, were sitting in the living room quietly discussing their day. Opa came home a few minutes later. As he opened the front door and before he could hang up his hat, he fell to the floor. Mother screamed, and Father pushed back his chair, rushing to Opa.

Hearing the commotion, Oma, Elga, and I ran from the kitchen into the living room. We stopped short when we saw Opa collapsed by the door. Father and Mother flew into a flurry of activity, checking Opa's heart rate, lungs, and pupils using medical terms I didn't understand. Reaching under Opa's arms, Father carefully dragged him into the first-floor bedroom as Mother guided his feet. They managed to get him onto their bed, easing the door shut behind them. Unable to help, Oma, Elga, and I stood in the living room frozen in silence.

I gathered up the courage to ask Oma, "What do you think is wrong with Opa?"

"I don't know," she whispered, wringing her hands and looking faint. Elga and I hurried to assist her into a chair. It was unbearable not knowing what was happening to Opa, and now we worried about Oma as well.

After what seemed like an hour, Father opened the bedroom door. Grave concern was etched on his face as he led Mother out of the room. Her shoulders slumped, her face ashen.

"Opa has had a stroke," Father announced. "We have made him comfortable, but he is in a coma."

All at once Oma cried out, "A gypsy fortune teller foretold it! She said misfortune would befall Opa in his 65th year, and it has come to pass!" She slumped over, sobbing uncontrollably. It was hard for us to see Oma so distraught. She was the beacon of light in our family, and a dark shadow had crossed her path.

Opa lay unresponsive in bed for several days. Oma was by his side without a moment's rest. They had been partners for over 40 years, and she wouldn't abandon him now.

Taking Elga and me aside, Father put his arms around us, warning, "If Opa wakes from his coma, the chances for his full recovery are not good. There could be significant damage to his mind as well as to his body."

I pulled back from Father's embrace and stared at him. Elga's hand flew to her mouth. How could Opa not recover? How could he not be the same Opa?

On one of Oma's rare breaks from Opa's bedside, Elga and I snuck into the bedroom. Opa's face was calm, his chest slightly rising and falling with each shallow breath. He looked like he was sleeping. Elga reached for Opa's hand, holding it while I whispered into his ear, my voice catching in my throat.

"Opa, please wake up. Oma needs you."

"We all need you," Elga added.

We heard footsteps approach and scurried out of the bedroom before Oma returned.

Then one evening toward the end of the week, we heard Oma's shouts from the bedroom.

"Praise the Lord. He's awake!"

We, along with Father and Mother, ran into the room. Opa stirred in his bed, his eyes open. With tears of gratitude, Oma sang praises to heaven and smothered him with kisses. We all rejoiced in the moment.

In the beginning, Opa was extremely weak. Oma worked with him daily to regain his speech and his strength to walk. However, Father was right to warn us. He was not the same. The stroke had dramatically changed his personality, leaving him fearful and agitated whenever Oma was out of his sight. He wasn't able to return to work. Music soothed him, but he couldn't play his instruments again. The loss of Opa's gift of music especially saddened us, but he was alive, and we cherished his presence.

⌁

In May of 1944, our little sister, Maija, was born. Mother spent a week in the hospital, and there were no complications. On the day of their scheduled return home, the slightest noise sent Elga and me scurrying to the front door, giddy with the anticipation of their arrival.

When Mother walked in, we ran to her. She carefully unwrapped the small wiggling bundle. "Biruta, look at her tiny pink fingers!" Elga gushed.

"I know, and look at her sweet little mouth," I replied. "Can we hold her?"

"Girls, don't crowd. Give Oma or Opa a chance to look at her, too," Mother grinned.

After Maija was passed around the family and admired, Elga and I bickered over whose turn it was to hold her next. Maija began to cry, and Mother reclaimed her.

"There has been enough excitement for one morning. I think Maija needs her rest. You'll both have plenty of opportunities to take care of her. There'll be unpleasant tasks too."

As if on cue, Maija spat up part of her last feeding.

"Ewww," Elga and I complained in unison as Oma and Opa laughed.

Father chuckled and winked at us.

Mother went back to work at the lab a few weeks later. Christina, our housekeeper from Alexander Heights, came in to help with Maija during the day. It freed Oma to work with Opa on his recovery. After school, Elga and I rushed home to assist Christina and Oma until our parents returned from work.

❧

In early June, the radio reported a major Allied victory in Normandy, France. The German troops were suffering more losses and continuing their retreat.

Late one afternoon, while gathering laundry from the clothesline in the backyard, I overheard a neighbor speaking to Father. They were talking over the wire fence that separated the two properties. There was a strain in their voices as they spoke about the startling developments in the war.

"With these major losses, I fear the German arr
be able to stop the Soviets from reclaiming the P
suffer again from their ruthless policies of impr'

deportation. We need to consider leaving Latvia," the neighbor said, stooping to pick up a blade of grass to chew on. "I hear the Germans are welcoming Baltic refugees into their country."

"I've heard the same," Father said, stroking his chin and thinking over what was said. "However, there's no certainty the Russians will return, and I can't help but think the German people are suffering in the war as well."

"That's true," the neighbor said, "but with the Communists knocking at our door again, we have to look at our options."

I quietly went back into the house with the basket of laundry. The discussion disturbed me, and I shared what I heard with Elga. That night, we noticed raised voices coming from our parents' bedroom. Father and Mother were having a heated conversation about our family's plans if the Soviets returned.

"Hermanis, you know our family was on the deportation list the first time the Communists were in Riga," Mother asserted. "By fate alone, they didn't find us because we were living in Mezparks. If they come back and conduct raids again, we won't be lucky enough to escape a second wave of deportations. We need to think about leaving. My parents and I are familiar with the language, and Germany seems like a viable option."

"I understand the dangers of staying here and agree we must consider leaving, but Germany?" Father argued. "I'm not as fluent in the language as you and your parents. The Germans started this miserable war. The living conditions there could be no better than here!"

"The war has caused no lack of physicians in all of Europe," Father continued, his voice rising. "Latvians are leaving for Sweden, England, Denmark, or anywhere else. Is it even urgent that we leave now? We don't even know for certain how close the Russians are."

There was a long pause. Elga and I gave each other worried looks, wondering what else would be said.

"Wait," Mother said. "What about Officer Rinne? He would know the situation better than us regarding the Soviets. I could find out what he knows."

After a few moments, Father's voice softened. "You're right, Elsa. At least he'll have more information to help us formulate a plan."

"I'll go to him tomorrow," Mother said.

We heard nothing further from our parents' room, and I let out my breath. Elga and I seldom heard our parents raise their voices to each other. I was relieved they had come to an agreement.

The following evening, Elga and I were in the kitchen helping to prepare dinner. Mother had just returned from work. She spoke to Father, who was sitting in the front room. Our ears perked up as they began to talk, and we edged closer to the door.

"Hermanis, the news is not good. Officer Rinne said the Russian troops have occupied much of the Latvian countryside and are approaching Riga. It's only a matter of weeks before they enter the city."

The sound of Father's chair scraping against the floor as he pushed it back, disclosed his alarm.

"I had no idea they were so close."

"There is more," Mother revealed. "He said that the German army is planning a retreat from Riga and urged us to leave as soon as possible."

"But where can we go on such short notice?"

Unnerved, Elga and I stood stock-still but leaned in closer to hear.

"Officer Rinne has proposed a solution," Mother said. "He suggested that we go to his residence in Altenburg, Germany, to live with Marianne, Sulli, and her grandmother. Because of the war, Officer Rinne and his son are rarely home. The women are alone in their large flat. If we lived there, it would provide them a sense of security as well as some needed income."

"Was he serious?" Father asked.

"Yes, Hermanis. He wants us to go. It's our only immediate plan to leave Riga."

"If the situation is as Officer Rinne describes, we'll need to take him up on his charitable offer."

It was an unexpected development. In the kitchen, Elga and I mouthed a silent scream. Not only would we be able to see Sulli again, but we would be living with her!

Nothing more was mentioned at the dinner table that night. However, later in the evening, Father and Mother spoke to Oma and Opa in private. The next morning our parents left the house early. We didn't see them again until dinner.

At the table, Oma ladled out a thin beet soup to everyone and passed around some coarse rye bread. When dinner was over, Elga and I glanced at each other, wondering whether Father and Mother would say anything.

Suddenly, Father cleared his throat.

"Girls, I think you've heard the latest news about the German losses in the war. Mother has found out from Officer Rinne that the Soviets are in Latvia and approaching Riga. We fear our family will be on the deportation list again if the Communists re-occupy the city. We've decided to leave."

Mother took a moment before adding, "Fortunately, Officer Rinne has made us a generous offer. He's suggested that our family stay with the Rinne family in Germany. Oma and Opa are aware of the plan and have agreed to come with us."

With solemn faces, Oma and Opa nodded their agreement.

At first, I looked at Elga and grinned. Then I glanced sideways at Oma and Opa. Opa's shoulders drooped, and Oma's chin quivered as she fought back tears. I hadn't thought about what leaving their home in Riga would mean to them. Elga and I had only been thinking about seeing Sulli again. A wave of guilt washed over me, and I lowered my eyes.

"There are still Communist sympathizers in the community who would report our leaving," Father said, looking at Elga and me. "So you mustn't talk about this with anyone, not even your friends. In these difficult times, it's hard to know whom to trust. Do you understand?"

"Yes, we understand."

"With the shortage of workers in Riga, Father's and my supervisors won't like the idea of our going and may not permit it," Mother explained. "But I didn't take the maternity leave that I was entitled to when Maija was born and will request it now. It will look as if our family is simply taking a brief holiday."

"But what about Oma and Opa's house?" Elga inquired.

"Christina, our housekeeper, will oversee the property while we're gone," Mother said.

"How will we get to the Rinnes?" I asked.

"I'm making those arrangements now," Father replied. "No matter how we go, it will take several days." He looked at us and added, "We'll need all your help with Maija and Opa."

"Of course," Elga said. "How long will we stay?"

Setting his jaw and turning to Oma and Opa, Father stated with conviction, "We will return to Riga when the war is over."

CHAPTER 7
Leaving

"By July 27, 1944, the Red Army had once again crossed the Latvian frontier...one of five Latvians fled their native land to escape the approaching Soviet hordes...There were now three main escape routes. One was overland through Lithuania and Poland into Germany. On another, small ships and boats were used to carry many Latvians to neutral Sweden...The third route, taken by most Latvians, was by German troop ships which carried Latvian refugees to Germany....This traffic also moved under a constant threat by Soviet naval and air units...Altogether some 300,000 Latvians, or about 20% of the population, left most or all of their property, dreams, and hopes to flee not only the ravages of war, but also the inhumanity of man." [6]

Mother was granted her leave from work, and Father secured passage for us on a boat to Danzig, Poland. We would make the remainder of the trip on trains, from Danzig to Berlin and Berlin to Altenburg, where the Rinnes lived.

"Isn't there a less complicated way to get to the Rinnes?" Mother asked Father. "The transfer from ship to train and to make yet another connection in Berlin will be a challenge with Maija and Opa. After all, she's only three months old, and Opa is just six months post-recovery from his stroke."

"I know, I worry about it as well, but there is no other way," Father said. "Many roads into Germany have been closed, and the land route is too long and treacherous. Besides, I wouldn't begin to know how to secure a vehicle to take all of us that distance. This is our only option."

"Isn't the Baltic Sea being patrolled by Soviet submarines? Is it safe to go by ship?"

Father heaved a heavy sigh and replied, "Elsa, there is a war going on, and there is no perfect route. It's our best option. Given what Officer Rinne has told us, we need to get our family out of Riga as soon as possible."

We began packing at once. As we sorted through our possessions, it pained me to see how much would be left behind. Almost everything we owned would be stored for an indefinite reunion as we traveled across a war-ravaged continent to safety. We would take only what we each could carry and have little more than the clothes on our backs.

Taking a break, I wandered into the living room where Opa sat at the piano. I watched him, unnoticed, as he stroked the keys without making a sound. He reached on top of the piano for the black case containing his silver flute. He opened it, lovingly running his fingers over the instrument. Tears glistened in his eyes as he clicked the case shut and returned it to its place. Respecting his private moment, I slipped out of the room.

I wandered into the kitchen where Oma was gathering foodstuffs and putting them in an empty two-gallon aluminum milk can for our journey. From her experiences during the first world war, she knew that food along the way would be limited. Nearby, Mother was folding diapers and baby clothes, layering them in the bottom of the basket to cushion the trip for our baby sister. A close friend of Mother's had made the basket to carry Maija.

Mother looked up to see me. "How are things going?" she asked.

"Okay," I replied. Mother continued to pack, so I listlessly moved on to the adjoining room.

Christina was filling a large wooden box to be shipped to the Rinne's address in Germany. It would be sent to us once she heard we had arrived in Altenburg. The crate was filled with warmer clothing, coats, blankets, and other items needed for the winter months. Taking it with us now would be unmanageable and give away our intent to stay away longer.

Later, Christina would pack up the rest of the household. Any items of precious or sentimental value to the family, like silverware or other non-essentials, would be shipped later. Furniture and larger objects would stay behind at the Mezparks house until we returned.

I went back upstairs, where Elga and I stowed the remainder of our room. I grabbed my sachel of childhood keepsakes and took it with me to stuff into one of the crates. We finished up and shuffled back to the kitchen where Oma and Mother were still packing.

"Now what can we do?" we asked with long faces.

In our younger years, whenever Elga and I were sad, Oma used to play a game with us. She would begin an imaginary story, and we, in turn, would create new lines adding to the story. Seeing our sullen expressions, Oma tried to lighten our mood.

She began, "Once upon a time…"

Elga and I looked at each other and snickered.

"Aren't we a little old for that game, Oma?" Elga asked.

"No," Mother said, "I think we all could use a little joy right now. How about, 'there was a loving family who lived happily in a peaceful land and¬…'"

"…suddenly a darkness fell over the land," Oma scowled with her hands stretched over her head like claws and continued, "and an evil emperor terrorized the country."

I couldn't help but laugh at Oma's pantomime and good-naturedly added, "The good family needed to escape the land or fall into the emperor's evil clutches."

I turned to look at Elga.

"Okay," Elga said, shrugging her shoulders, not sure she wanted to play along. "The family heard about a magical kingdom and fled for their safety."

"Once there, they found their faithful friend, Sulli…" Mother added.

"… and together they built a magnificent castle in the magical kingdom and lived happily ever after," Oma ended.

For a brief moment, the thinly veiled story about our family's upcoming journey lifted our spirits, and we all burst out laughing.

"See," Oma said, "We should all look at this as a new adventure with new possibilities."

That evening before our departure, Father and Mother called Elga and me into the living room. Mother sat on the piano bench, facing us while Father stood staring out the window, rubbing the back of his neck.

We sat down on the sofa, and I noticed Mother fidgeting with the wedding band on her finger.

"We leave tomorrow because the Soviets are about to re-enter Riga," she said.

I flashed Elga a confused look. We knew the reason for our family's departure. Why was Mother reminding us again?

Father turned away from the window but paced in front of it. He spoke to us while looking at the floor.

"And I'm sure you remember our close brush with deportation a few years ago," he said.

I squirmed in my seat. The anxiety in the room was palpable and unsettling. I knew Father and Mother had finalized all the arrangements for our travel, and we would be staying with the Rinnes. I didn't understand their unease.

Father stopped pacing and turned to look at Elga and me.

"I'm not going with the family to Germany."

I drew in a sharp breath, the air catching in my throat, "What?!"

"Why?" Elga asked, glaring at Father. "It doesn't make any sense."

Father swung back toward the window, gazing out with an empty stare.

"The ships are only transporting women, children, and the elderly to Germany. All able-bodied men are required to stay behind to assist with the German army's evacuation."

In a dull tone, Father lowered his head and added, "I

attempted to get an exemption because of Maija and Opa, but it was of no use."

Father went to the piano bench to sit next to Mother. He put his arm around her shoulders but continued addressing us.

"Biruta, Elga both of you will have a bigger responsibility in helping the family get to Germany."

Elga and I went to them, and we all held hands for a moment, taking in the new development.

"We'll help, of course," Elga said, breaking the silence, "but we can't do it without you, Father."

"Yes. You can. Your Mother is a strong woman, and you are both strong young women as well," Father said. "I have confidence you'll be able to help Mother manage the situation."

"But Father! How will you get to Germany?" I asked in a panic.

"I'm leaving my position at the German health department and taking a position as a laborer on one of the evacuating troop ships. When I get to Germany, I will come to find you at the Rinne's."

I paused, quietly assessing our situation. On the upcoming voyage, there would be six of us: Mother, carrying three-month-old Maija; Opa, emotionally dependent on Oma since his stroke and both in their mid-sixties; and Elga and I, just over 14 years old. Without Father's assistance and protection, I knew the challenges we faced would be daunting, even dangerous. The fairy tale we had spun earlier with Oma had been a fool's dream. I wasn't sure there was a happy ending.

～★

As word spread of the Soviets approaching Riga, city transportation became disrupted as many planned to leave.

Father needed to find a way to get our family, along with our luggage, across town to the port. A former patient of Father's had a horse and wagon. He lived near the harbor and offered to take us and provide lodging at his home the night before we sailed. Father accepted.

The day before our family was scheduled to leave, I drifted through the first floor of our grandparents' home, lingering briefly in each room. I was sad, recalling the many happy times that had occurred within its walls. I went upstairs to our bedroom and looked outside at *liela priede* and the other tall pine trees in the yard. For one last time, I inhaled their fresh aromatic scent. I glanced down the street toward the entrance to the zoo and, in my mind's eye could see it and the lake beyond it. I smiled, remembering our summers in Mezparks.

When the cart arrived later in the afternoon, we gathered our things and shuffled toward the front door. Oma was giving Christina last-minute instructions regarding the house. We filed past Christina as we left, hugging her with our heartfelt good-byes, not knowing when we would return.

Father took Maija in her basket to the wagon while Mother, Oma, Opa, Elga, and I each carried our luggage. We loaded our few belongings in the back of the cart and sat next to them on benches. Father sat up front with the driver.

Each clip-clop of the horse's hooves on the pavement took us further from our lives in Mezparks. Going past Alexander Heights, my overall gloom intensified as childhood memories came flooding back. The wagon continued weaving along the city streets, making its way toward the harbor. We would stay with the driver and his family overnight, getting up at dawn to go to our ship.

In the early morning of August 8, 1944, our family arose to dense morning fog. The gray skies matched my mood. We re-entered the wagon for the short distance to the docks. Sitting in the rear, I studied each family member's solemn face as we rode in silence. Even Maija was quiet in her basket. I gazed at Father's back and saw his slumping shoulders as he sat next to the driver. I closed my eyes to keep happier thoughts of Father ingrained in my memory. A short while later, the horse stopped, and I could see we were at the port.

In the thinning fog, the family delayed a few moments to take in the harbor scene before getting out and unloading our things. Through the mist, we made out the outlines of the re-purposed troop ship rolling on the dark waves of the Baltic Sea. It would take us to Poland.

Nearby, a line of passengers was forming to be taken out to the anchored ship. The ship's smaller boats, the tenders, approached the pier to ferry passengers across to the anchored vessel. Numbed by the damp and chilly morning air, I shivered as our family joined the line. As we inched closer toward boarding, people around us embraced their loved ones and cried. My throat tightened, realizing we, too, would be soon saying good-bye to Father.

After we had found out Father wasn't coming with us to Germany, the family had spent as much time together as we could. Now that the actual moment of departure was upon us, the heartache we felt was worn on our faces. If we only knew when Father would be joining us in Germany, the pain of leaving without him would be more bearable.

When it was Mother's time to board, Father firmly grasped her in a long embrace and whispered in her ear. Letting her go, he kissed her and then leaned over to kiss

Maija in the basket before they entered the boat. He then embraced Oma and Opa, in turn, hugging them and giving his blessings for the journey.

Lastly, Father turned to Elga and me. He tried to remain stoic, but I saw him mop at the corner of his eyes with a sleeve before reaching out to wrap his arms around us. I clung to Father, afraid to let him go. A tear slid down my cheek.

"Isn't there any way you can be with us?" I rasped, barely able to speak.

Equally distraught, Elga sputtered, "Father, can't you please come along?"

"Biruta, Elga, you know how much I want to be with you, but I can't," Father said in anguish. "You must both stay strong to help Mother until I see you again in Germany."

He held on to us for a moment before kissing us on the forehead and directing us toward Mother, Maija, Oma, and Opa, already on the tender. Elga and I found a seat, positioning ourselves to look at Father for as long as we could when we left the dock.

I will never forget how Father looked as he stood on the pier. Clenching his jaw, lines of despair creased his haggard face. My heart sank. Despite knowing we would be leaving Father behind, up until that very moment, I hadn't fully acknowledged the agony and uncertainty of our separation. There was a possibility we would never see each other again.

Elga and I gave Father a wave, trying to reassure him we would be all right, but emotions overcame me. I wanted to stay brave for Father, but tears spilled down my cheeks. I turned to look at Elga's damp face and reached for her hand.

The tender revved its engines to pull away from the pier. We stretched out our arms, reaching toward Father, and he blew us kisses in return. The boat backed out into the open harbor and then forged ahead. Elga and I turned our heads to see Father's silhouette blend into the crowd of family members left standing on the dock. Spent from crying, Elga and I wiped our tears and held onto each other as we watched the harbor melt into Riga's skyline.

CHAPTER 8
Beginning the Journey

O ur boat bounced ahead on steely blue waves of the harbor, to the vessel that would take us to Danzig, Poland. As we approached the ship, it loomed before us. It dwarfed the tender as we bobbed next to it like a small cork on the water. At sea level, the smooth metal sides of the ship's hull kept us from clearly seeing the upper decks. Straining my neck to look up, it took my breath away. I had never been close to anything so massive and wondered how it would keep us afloat.

The sailors on the ship burst into a flurry of activity preparing for our boarding. I watched as they lowered a gangplank, the length of a long ladder, from an entrance in the ship's hull to our tender. The crewmen struggled to attach the walkway to our small boat lurching in the sea swells. The gangplank, steep and loosely tethered, swayed with the rhythm of the waves churning below it. Our only aids in crossing were evenly spaced horizontal boards to secure one's footing and worn rope handrails on either side of the plank. Realizing this was how we would be boarding, my knees went weak.

Fear replaced thoughts of Father and Riga. A sailor stationed at the foot of the gangplank and another by the entrance were available for assistance. One-by-one, passengers grabbed onto the rope handrail and stepped onto the careening walkway, staggering up toward the ship. Panic seized me as I realized Mother's hands weren't free to hold onto the handrails. She was holding the basket with Maija in it.

When it was Mother's turn to cross, she alerted the sailor to her need for help with the basket. He approached, and she showed him Maija inside. He motioned for her to give him the basket. Just as she was ready to hand Maija to him, a passenger in the tender shouted out.

"Don't let him do it! I've heard a baby was lost to the sea when the sailor dropped the child!"

Mother stood frozen, holding the basket mid-air between herself and the sailor. I held my breath, not knowing what she would do.

The sailor had heard the passenger's warning. With chin held high, he looked directly into Mother's eyes. He waited for her to hand Maija to him. Pressing her lips together tightly and focusing on the sailor, Mother handed the basket over to him, entrusting Maija into his care.

Skillfully, the sailor crossed the gangplank and passed the basket up to the second sailor at the ship's entrance. Mother switfly crossed. Once onboard, she retrieved Maija's basket and turned back to smile at the sailor. The passengers on the tender cheered. Then she gestured for the rest of our family to board.

Later, the passenger who had warned Mother asked her

why she had trusted the sailor. Mother's response has always stayed with me.

"Like our leaving Riga, I was forced to act by circumstance, not by choice," she answered.

Seeing that Maija and Mother were safe, I relaxed but only for a moment. I saw Opa in line to go next. Oma informed the sailor about Opa's recent stroke. Acknowledging her concern, the sailor walked behind Opa, hands on his waist, to steady him. I placed my hands over my eyes, only partially watching as they crossed. The sailor returned to assist Oma, who took her time making small, cautious steps. Following her, Elga held her head high, barely touching the ropes, and scampered over the span. I was next.

"C'mon, Biruta! You can do it!" Elga yelled from the ship. "Don't look down!"

Instantly my eyes were drawn to the water, and every limb in my body shook with fear. My eyes shot back up to Elga, building my confidence. Taking a deep breath and holding it in, I grasped the rope handrails. With determination, I planted my first step on the plank and with long strides went across. Upon reaching the entrance, I frantically grabbed for the sailor's hand to help me up. Once inside, I blew out my breath.

"I made it!" I shouted to my family standing nearby. We were finally all onboard.

Inside the ship, we retrieved our luggage that had been loaded earlier. Ship personnel then guided the passengers down below to a narrow passageway. Near the center of the ship, the women and children were shown to their quarters. One large room held dozens of bunk beds for our overnight voyage. The men's quarters were in a different area toward the rear of the ship. Realizing Opa would be separated from us,

Mother objected. She explained to the staff about his stroke and dependency on Oma. However, no exceptions were made. As Opa was taken away with the other men, he reached out, whimpering for Oma.

Wringing her hands, Oma cried, "Oh, no! What are we going to do?"

"I'm afraid there is nothing we can do," Mother replied, placing one arm around Oma's shoulders. "We'll check in on Opa as soon as we can."

With no recourse, we settled into one corner of the room and stowed our few belongings for the journey. Mother took a lower bunk setting Maija's basket beside her. Oma took a lower bunk as well while Elga and I took beds above them.

A short time later, a deep, mournful bellow of the ship's horn signaled our departure. The engines began to clank and churn, and the smell of diesel fuel permeated the room. The ship left the harbor and began to sway on the sea's undulating waves. The motion and the smell nauseated Elga and me. Oma worried about Opa, and the three of us decided to find him and get some fresh air. Mother stayed behind with Maija.

When we found the men's quarters and Opa saw us, he beamed from ear-to-ear. Despite the trauma of separating from us, he seemed well. Relieved to see Opa safe and at ease, Oma smiled and took his hand, leading him out into the ship's hallway.

We looked for a way to get to an upper deck to escape the diesel odors and found a stairway leading outside. We climbed a flight of stairs and opened the door. Lifeboats and artillery were affixed to the flooring, leaving us little room to walk around. The ship was a military transport taking troops to the front and returning refugees to Germany. We wound our way around the equipment to stand at a railing and gaze out over the Baltic Sea, inhaling the fresh sea breezes.

It seemed like just a short while ago that we left Father in Riga, but the sun was already high above us. It reflected a wide golden swath on the stretch of sea before us. A fine spray rising from the ship's wake misted my face. I wrinkled my nose at the salty feel and scent of the sea air. At least it was better than the stench of diesel fuel below. Despite the rolling waves, the vast sea seemed peaceful. It was hard to imagine the world was at war.

After a brief time enjoying the view, we walked Opa back to the men's area and returned to our quarters. Shortly after, an announcement came over the ship's intercom. Food was being served in the mess hall. Mother and Oma went to get Opa and find it. Elga and I stayed behind with Maija.

We entertained ourselves making funny faces at Maija in her basket. She smiled and kicked, making us laugh. Elga and I took turns holding and rocking her in our arms until she fell asleep. With nothing else to do, we climbed onto our beds and laid down face up, our hands clasped behind our heads.

"I wonder what Father is doing right now," Elga sighed.

"Yeah. I miss him already, too."

After a few quiet moments, she mused, "I wonder what it will be like living in Germany with Sulli."

"If it's like our time together in Riga, it'll be great. Do you think our German will be good enough to get by?" I asked.

"I don't know, but we'll soon find out."

Several minutes later, Mother and Oma returned. They had located the mess hall and encouraged us to go. Elga and I weren't hungry. The ship's rhythmic swaying and the diesel odors still left our stomachs unsettled. We noticed some passengers suffered more. Many went to the top deck to hang over the rails or rushed to find the bathrooms for relief. I spent the rest of the afternoon and evening in my bunk. Later, when physical and emotional exhaustion overcame me, I fell asleep.

The next morning, I awoke feeling better. I no longer noticed the smell of diesel, and the sway of the ship almost soothed me. Perhaps I was becoming accustomed to a life at sea.

At the end of our second day, we made port in Danzig. Even though I had gotten used to the movement of the ship, it felt good to have my feet on solid ground again. From the port, our family needed to go to the train station less than a mile away. It was a distance we could easily walk. However, we had Maija in her basket and six articles to transport from the port to the train station.

Mother devised a system. On the first walk to the train station, Mother would carry Maija in her basket and the food can. Oma and Opa would go along, each bringing their own bags. Elga and I would stay behind at the port to watch over the rest of our things. Once at the train station Oma, Opa, and Maija would remain while Mother returned to the port for Elga and me. Then the three of us would go to the train station with the rest of our luggage.

"I feel like a mother cat moving her kittens," Mother laughed as the three of us walked to the station. Then a somber expression crossed her face.

"I realized as I watched the other refugees, we really didn't need to guard our things so carefully."

Elga and I gave Mother puzzled looks, not understanding what she was trying to say.

"No one traveling at this time thinks about taking anyone else's belongings," she explained with a bitter sigh. "Everyone realizes and respects that the few things we each carry are the only possessions we still have."

Once we were all together at the train station, Mother's fluency in German made it easy for her to purchase our tickets and find our connection to Berlin. The train was full, and we jostled to find seats together. Managing to secure them and arranging our bags, we settled in for the scheduled day-long journey. The train whistle blew, and clouds of steam escaped from the engine as the train chugged ahead. I blew the air from my lungs and breathed a little easier.

My relief was short-lived. As the train headed toward Berlin, chilling signs of war flashed by the train's windows. Mud-caked military equipment on flatbed rail cars caused our train to stop frequently, allowing them to pass. Military equipment returning from the front took priority over evacuating refugees.

What was more unsettling; however, were the frequent sightings of Allied bombers. The train stopped when they appeared, and a siren wailed, signaling the passengers to get off. Everyone scrambled, leaving their belongings behind – except Oma, who always took her container of food with her.

We hid in ditches with our hands covering our heads as the planes flew over. I was terrified, and my heart pounded until the all-clear signal was given. No bombs ever dropped near us. However, as we approached Berlin, the warnings came more often, delaying our arrival. Our one day trip stretched to nearly two, and by the time we arrived at our destination, our nerves were shattered.

When we got to the Berlin train station, it was much larger than Danzig's. The Berlin station would have been challenging to manage in quieter times, but this was sheer pandemonium. The six members of our family were just a drop in the sea of humanity converging here. I looked around in amazement, surrounded by a crush of frustrated people with voices clamoring in several different languages. Refugees must have come here from every corner of Europe. Everyone was hustling to make their connections while keeping track of their family members and their belongings.

Poor Opa was completely disoriented, clinging tightly to Oma, fearful of being separated from her again. Elga and I struggled to hold onto Maija's basket to prevent it from toppling onto the busy train station floor while Mother went to get our tickets for the final leg of our journey.

Once she had the tickets, Mother led the way to find our train to Altenburg. Pushing our way through the bustling crowds, we boarded our train and secured two small train compartments; one for Oma and Opa and one for us.

Relieved to escape the chaos of the station, we climbed on board. Taking our seats, we unwound in the quieter space of the train car. Mother returned to the station to wire the Rinnes to let them know we were arriving from Berlin that evening.

We had left Riga four days ago, and it was another half a day south to Altenburg, a community of 44,000 people. Sulli and her mother would meet us at the station. Fatigue overpowered my excitement to see them. Once the train left the station, I slept until I was jarred awake by the train jolting to a stop in Altenburg.

Rubbing my eyes, I looked outside. It was early evening. Searching the platform for Sulli and her mother, I saw them scanning the passengers as they left the train. From inside, Elga and I waved to get Sulli's attention, but she didn't see us.

Our family gathered our luggage and hurried toward the exit. Tired of traveling, but refreshed from my brief rest, my excitement returned. I couldn't wait to see Sulli and get to her home. As we stepped off the train, Sulli immediately saw Elga and me and came running toward us.

"You're finally here!" she shouted, and the three of us threw ourselves into a collective hug.

"Well, it's good to see you're glad to be together again," Marianne said, grinning.

She turned to greet Oma and Opa and then kissed Mother on the cheek.

"We're happy you've all made it here safely," she said. She took Maija's basket from Mother's hands and peered inside. "I see you have a new family member."

"I want to see too!" Sulli exclaimed, running over to take a look. Cooing at Maija, she said, "You're so cute! You'll certainly liven things up at our house."

We all laughed and began the short walk from the train station to the Rinne's residence. I didn't mind the walk and strolled with a bounce in my step.

～

The Rinnes lived in a three-story apartment building with one flat taking up each of the floors. The landlords, a physician and his wife, lived on the second floor. The physician-husband had been called to the German front and hadn't been home for some time. His wife was left to manage the building. The third floor, currently not in use, had been the doctor's office.

Sulli, her mother, and grandmother lived on the first floor. Sulli's father and her older brother, both in the German army were rarely home. Marianne had the women's beds moved into the dining room, the largest sunlit room. It stayed warmer there during the winter months. They closed off the empty rooms to save on heating costs.

Mother and Maija, and Oma and Opa were given two small rooms off the dining room that appeared, at one time, to have been servant quarters. Elga and I took two couches in a large sitting room adjacent to the dining room. The emotional intensity of the last five days had taken its toll and I struggled to stay awake. My head hit the pillow and I promptly fell asleep.

The next day, I woke up alert. Pulling out clean clothes from my suitcase, I took my turn in the bathroom. I tore off the clothing I had worn for the last several days, drew a bath, and soaked from head to toe in privacy. Fully refreshed, I walked into the kitchen. The Rinnes and my family were seated and eating a light breakfast of bread and ersatz coffee made from roasted grains. Real coffee hadn't been available since the war began.

After we had eaten, Mother wrote to Father and Christina to let them know we had arrived at the Rinnes. We had no idea when they would receive our post, but we hoped our message would get through.

It had been two years since Sulli had stayed with us. Eager to catch up with each other, Sulli, Elga, and I wandered into our makeshift bedroom.

Straight away, Sulli confided, "I was so happy to see you last night, but I have to admit that when I first saw all of you, I was in shock. You truly looked like a group of vagabonds." Grinning, she added, "You look much better now."

Imagining how we must have appeared as we stepped off the train, Elga and I smiled, accepting Sulli's ribbing.

Our conversation then turned to the war and how it had disrupted our families' lives. We told Sulli how unexpected and sad it was to leave Father behind in Riga. With the situation in Latvia uncertain, we also worried if Father would make it out of Riga before the Soviets arrived. If he did, we were concerned about how he would get to the Rinnes.

Sulli was troubled, too, about her father's safety. He was a supply officer for the German army and always worked close to the front. She and her family also stressed about her brother, never knowing where he was stationed. Before the war, her brother had wanted to go to law school but was drafted into the German army immediately out of high school. It reminded Elga and me of the young German soldiers who stayed with us in Mezparks a few years ago. The three of us fell silent with the thoughts of the family members who weren't with us.

❧

School was starting, and Elga and I would be attending high school with Sulli. She introduced us to her best friends, Anneliese and Ingetraud, also known as Teddy.

"We're so happy to meet you," Elga said, "but to be honest, Biruta and I are a little worried about attending a German high school."

"Our general knowledge of the language is okay," I explained, "but not at a high school level. I don't know how we'll ever get through reading literature and writing essays in German."

"Don't worry," Annelise said, "we'll all be glad to help, and it will be fun to study together."

"Besides, most of the teachers are kind and very understanding," Teddy added.

"See, I told you not to worry," Sulli said with a smile. "It's a good school, and I have great friends."

Once classes began, an older math teacher soon realized Elga and I were foreign students and took us under his wing. He was supportive and concerned not only for us but for all his students.

On a crisp, clear night, he invited the entire class for an evening lesson in astronomy. He made it enjoyable to learn about the major constellations of Cassiopeia, Orion, Gemini, and the twin stars Castor and Pollux.

Looking up at the stars, I wished not only for Father and Officer Rinnes' safe return to us, but also for peace. Despite the war and all its hardships, the evidence of a larger universe comforted me. It reminded me that there were people, like the Rinnes and our teacher, who remained thoughtful, kind, and committed to helping others. It gave me hope in our humanity.

❦

Almost two months after our arrival in Altenburg, the large wooden crate Oma and Christina had packed in Mezparks arrived at the Rinnes. With the excitement of Christmas, we all gathered around it, and Mother pried the lid free. Once open, Opa instantly recognized the small black case resting on top. Joy radiated from his face as he opened the case to see his cherished silver flute. He assembled its pieces to blow a single wavering note.

Oma smiled at Opa, her eyes glistening. She turned back to the crate, and her smile broadened when she saw that Christina had thought to pack her embroidery materials as well. I saw my satchel of keepsakes and grabbed it, clutching it close to my heart. Crowding closer to look into the crate, we were excited to see what other "forgotten" contents the shipment contained.

Mother stopped, and her eyes widened as she noticed a letter in Father's distinct handwriting placed on top of his clothing. She grabbed the letter, ripping the envelope open to read it out loud.

My Dearest Elsa and darling daughters,

> *Greetings to Oma and Opa and my warmest regards to the Rinnes for sharing their home with you in Altenburg. I pray all of you are safe and well. I only have a moment to write before shipping these items.*
>
> *I am leaving soon on a ship to Germany. We are loading machinery out of Riga to transport to Bremerhaven. I am unsure when we arrive or if I will be discharged after we unload the shipment at the port. I calculate it is about 300 miles south to Altenburg. I will do everything in my power to get to you as soon as I can.*
>
> *I miss you all dearly and think about you every minute of every day. I look forward to seeing your smiling faces and holding you all in my arms again soon.*

All My Love,
Father

"He's coming to Germany!" Elga and I shrieked in unison.

We finally had word that Father would be arriving. We were so excited to hear from him that no one dared to say out loud what we had heard over the radio. The Soviets had increased their submarine patrols on the Baltic Sea. Over the last two months, several German ships had been sunk by torpedoes and submerged mines. Father's crossing would be much more perilous than ours had been.

CHAPTER 9
Altenburg | 1944 - 1945

D ays turned into weeks, and then more than a month passed since we had received Father's letter. The family listened intently to the daily radio broadcasts for news about ship activity on the Baltic Sea. However, had a ship been sunk, its type, location, or origin wasn't disclosed. The Germans weren't open about reporting their losses. We ached to hear any word from Father, but all we could do was hope and pray that he was not on any of those ill-fated ships.

One bright, pleasant afternoon, Elga and I, along with Sulli, Annelise, and Teddy, were walking home from school. We were teasing Sulli about a good-looking boy in math class who was paying a lot of attention to her.

"One plus one equals two," we giggled, puckering our lips and making kissing sounds at Sulli.

At first, Sulli laughed along with us, but as the teasing wore thin, she scowled and became sullen. We changed the subject and stopped under the shadows of an apple tree across the street from Sulli's house to talk about school and our classmates.

In the distance, we saw a bicycle approaching. A typical way to travel at the time, we thought nothing of it. As it neared, we saw a grizzled man in rumpled clothing riding a dilapidated bike. Stopping every so often to straddle his bicycle, he looked over the handlebars to check the house numbers on the doorposts.

Curious, we watched the bedraggled bicyclist pause in front of the Rinne flat. He took out a slip of paper from his pocket and checked the address. At first unaware of us, but then sensing someone watching, he turned around to see us standing under the shadows of the tree. He stepped off his bicycle, letting it drop and walked toward us, studying our faces.

Frightened and taken off guard, we all took a step back further into the shadows, distancing ourselves from the strange man and remaining silent.

"Biruta, Elga? Is it you? I can't believe I've found you."

The voice was familiar, but the grizzled features were not. He looked heavenward and then back at us.

In a voice filled with emotion, he said, "It's me, Father."

It took a moment for us to recognize the smiling blue eyes behind the weary, unshaven face.

"Father!" Elga and I shouted.

He opened his arms to wrap us in his embrace, and we rushed at him, nearly toppling him over. We stood like that for a very long time.

"We thought we'd never see you again!" Elga cried into his shoulder.

"We were afraid you might have gone down on a ship!" I added through my tears.

"Well, I'm here now in flesh and blood with both of you," Father said as he nuzzled us. Then he abruptly pulled away.

"Where's Mother and Maija? And Opa and Oma? Is everyone alright?"

Knowing the rest of the family was inside, Elga and I shouted as loudly as we could to an open window on the first floor. "Mother, come quick! Father's here!"

A second later, Mother looked out the window. "Biruta, Elga! What's going on? Why are you both shouting?"

Then she saw a strange man holding onto us, and her face went white.

Mother stood rigid, first in fear, and then in disbelief as she studied the features of the man's face.

"It's Father!" Elga and I shouted.

Mother let out a cry and disappeared from the window. In a flash, she was out the front door and into Father's arms. She pulled away from him, looked into his eyes, and spoke to him in a rush of words.

"When we hadn't heard from you in weeks, we were worried sick! Ships were reported sunk on the Baltic, and we feared the worst!"

Mother folded back into his arms. They stood there a while longer until she broke from his embrace and stepped back.

"Hermanis, let's all go inside. You must need food and drink, and then we want to hear how you got here and why it's taken so long."

The four of us strolled toward the flat when Mother paused at the front door.

"Hermanis, do you have any idea what day it is tomorrow?"

"No, Elsa, my dear. I've been traveling on the back roads of Germany for weeks. I've completely lost track of the days."

"It's November 18th," she said.
Recognizing the date, Father's face winced in irony.
"It's Latvian Independence Day."

⤙⤚

After Father had an opportunity to unwind and refresh himself, we pressed him about his travels from Riga to Altenburg. He settled into a chair and began to share the details of his journey.

After Father had written his letter to us, he worked several days loading heavy machinery onto a transport ship that would take him to Germany. He was aware of the increased dangers on the Baltic Sea, but his ship made it through without incident. Arriving in Bremerhaven, it was unclear whether he would be released from his job. While unloading the transport, a cargo of heavy equipment rolled over his toe, breaking it. It was a misfortune, but got him discharged.

Altenburg was 300 miles southeast of the port, and Father began looking for ways to get to us. Traveling on the main throughways would be dangerous. Allied planes patrolled the major transportation routes, ready to bomb or machine-gun anything that moved on them.

Walking the back roads, Father only carried a spare change of clothing, stuffing his identification papers and his final salary in his shirt. Sometimes he'd wave down a local farmer, but finding a ride was challenging, and traveling this way was slow. At night, he'd sleep wherever he could find cover. Sometimes, he got a farmer's permission to sleep in their haylofts. Other times, he slept in hayfields or on a cushion of pine needles in the forest. He ate berries along the way or used some of his money to buy bread as he passed through the villages. At the sound of an airplane, he dove into the ditches or ran into the forest, doing what he could to remain unseen.

While walking on the outskirts of a small village, Father had a stroke of luck. He noticed an old bicycle discarded a few yards from the side of the road. He inspected it and found that it hadn't been badly damaged. With a few nuts and bolts and proper oiling, he felt it could be salvaged.

Nearby, Father noticed a home with a few scattered farm implements in the yard and a small shed in the back. He hoped the owner would grant him access to the shed and that parts and tools were inside.

Father gathered his courage and knocked on the front door of the house. A suspicious man, a little older than himself, cracked the door open. Father explained to him in broken German, that he needed to repair the bike to get to his family in Altenburg. After piecing together Father's story, the man was sympathetic and willing to help, showing Father to the shed.

Father spent the better part of a day working on the bicycle, the man watching him cobble it together and lending him advice. Toward evening, the bike was repaired. Father rode it up and down the road a few times, testing it until he felt satisfied. Returning to the shed, the man slapped Father on the back in congratulatory praise.

"If only for a few hours, the gentleman and I were able to leave the war behind us. It was gratifying to work together toward a common cause," Father said and then continued with his story.

Darkness set in. The man offered Father food and shelter, telling him he was welcome to sleep in the shed for the night.

Father was happy to have a home-cooked meal and a roof over his head.

The following morning, the man's wife made him breakfast. Father offered the couple money for their kindness, but they refused, wishing him well on his mission to find us. They said their goodbyes, and with his newly functioning bicycle, Father went on his way. He knew he could make several more miles a day riding than on foot.

In the late morning of his second week, Father made it to the city outskirts of Leipzig. Stopping to ask for directions, he was thrilled to discover he was less than 30 miles away from Altenburg. Relieved, he bought some lunch and rested before making his final push to reach us.

"Several miles into my ride, the vague outlines of a town appeared in the distance. With each mile I pedaled, the skyline became clearer and clearer. I knew it must be Altenburg," Father said. "My heart began pounding faster and faster, and I prayed the bike would hold together until I found you.

I heard about the worsening conditions in Germany and didn't know if you had received my letter. I had no idea if you were alright. The only thing that kept me going was my desire to see all of you again."

Overcome with emotion, Father couldn't speak and waved his hand to shoo away the unthinkable thoughts. Taking in a deep breath, he went on.

"It doesn't matter. I'm here now and want to hear how you've been doing. How was your trip to Germany?"

Since we had come upon Father first, Elga and I felt entitled to tell our family's story. Rushing our words, we interrupted each other, sharing how we had boarded the ship, the air raids on the train, and the crowded train station in Berlin. We told

Father about our new friends and experiences in a German high school.

"My! You've experienced a lot!" Father exclaimed, shaking his head. "You've had your own adventure!"

Shifting his position to look at Mother, Father asked, "And what about you, Elsa? How have the rest of you managed?"

"Since our arrival, we've gotten into a routine," Mother said. "There's rationing, of course, and a scarcity of food, but we combine resources with the Rinnes. Grandmother Rinne and Oma have been creative in making ends meet."

"I could have easily gotten work here," Mother continued. "Many physicians here have been called to the front, and few are left in the city. Maija is still young, so I've decided to stay at home. In many ways, it's been a blessing. I'm still nursing her and am entitled to extra food rations because of it."

Mother sighed, shaking her head, "I'm required to go to a control station to weigh Maija both before and after her feedings to justify the extra rations. I can't believe the absurdities of war!

But I do have news that may be of interest to you, Hermanis," Mother said, her eyes gleaming.

She told Father about the vacant doctor's office on the third floor that belonged to the landlady's husband. Like other physicians in the city, he was abruptly called to the German front. The office was still fully supplied, waiting for his eventual return.

Father's face lit up at the news, "Do you think the landlady would allow me to work there?"

With a broad smile, Mother replied, "I'm not sure, but there's no harm in asking."

The very next morning, Father talked to the landlady and returned to tell us what she said.

"I sensed there was some hesitation. After all, it is her husband's office. However, she knows of the scarcity of physicians in town and will rent it to me for a reasonable price until her husband returns."

Beaming, Father grabbed Mother by the shoulders and declared, "I'll be able to work!"

It only took a few weeks for Father to obtain the necessary authorizations. He posted his office hours in the local paper and word spread. In no time, Father was seeing patients.

An oil refinery on the outskirts of Altenburg was also looking for a part-time physician. The refinery needed an on-call doctor for employee accidents, which occurred on site. Father inquired and got the job.

There was one complication. The refinery was a short distance outside of town. Although the refinery would provide a car, Father had always relied on public transportation and had never learned to drive. Desperate for his services, the refinery manager assigned Father a car and driver. By coincidence, the driver was another Latvian refugee, Janis Bremanis.

Janis and his wife, Aina, were professional symphony musicians. He was a violinist and his wife, a harpist. They sold their home to buy a car and escaped Latvia early when the roads to Germany were still open. The car provided them the security of transporting Aina's harp and Janis's violin safely.

The Bremanis' musical talents weren't needed during the war, but Janis's ability to drive and his possession of a car made him employable. Fate had brought Janis and Father together. Their bond as fellow Latvians and their drives together to the refinery forged a lasting friendship between them.

The refinery was a dangerous place to work. Not only were there routine accidents and injuries from the machinery, but it was also a frequent Allied bombing target. The plant supplied precious fuel not only to the German people, but more importantly, for the German army.

One evening in the middle of the night, Father was summoned to the refinery. He was needed to tend to casualties following an Allied bombing. Days later, German locals marveled at the Allied intelligence, wondering how they had known the refinery had been rebuilt following a recent attack.

～✒

Christmas 1944 arrived. The holiday was a somber one. Officer Rinne returned home on leave but was soon called away to attend to his critically ill mother. For weeks, there had been no word about Sulli's brother.

Christmas Eve dinner consisted of a simple meal of rye bread and cabbage soup. Afterward, we went to the living room to exchange modest gifts we had made for each other. Blackout curtains hung in the windows, darkening the room. Only a single candle provided any light.

I made a calendar for the Rinne family that I had created in art class at school. Although Sulli's mother raved at my artistry, I was embarrassed when Sulli's grandmother gently pointed out that I had misspelled the German word for "Christmas" on the calendar.

After we exchanged gifts and hugs, the room became silent. Somewhere in the distance, the sound of airplane engines droned overhead. Was it possible there would be bombings on Christmas Eve? Or were they passing us over for bigger targets? We held our breaths waiting for the sirens fearing we might need to flee for the safety of the basement. However, the droning faded, and no air raid sirens sounded.

We sat quietly until Oma broke the silence, saying, "Up to now, the Lord has blessed us with his great kindness."

I reflected on Oma's words. She was right, of course. Over the past year, our family had experienced many kindnesses. We had all escaped the Soviets and arrived to Altenburg without harm. Living with friends, we had a roof over our heads, and Father was employed. We had food, although meager, on the table and were all still alive.

No one spoke for several minutes. Then one-by-one, in the flickering candlelight of the darkened room, we talked about the things for which we were thankful. After everyone had spoken, we prayed and sang, "Stille Nacht".

The peace we experienced on Christmas Eve didn't last. In an effort to end the war, the Allies stepped up their bombing campaign in Germany a few days after Christmas.

Things deteriorated. Evening curfew hours were extended and more strictly enforced. At night, everything went eerily dark. No street lamps or car headlights were allowed, and blackout curtains were required in every window.

Nothing moved on the streets after dusk except authorized military and medical personnel. The only noise we heard after dark was the intermittent sound of airplanes flying overhead. We became numb to the air raid sirens and robotically ran for shelter when we heard them.

One evening in the middle of the night, the air raid sirens wailed. Familiar with the routine, we jumped from our beds and ran to the basement of our building. Huddled underground, we sat on edge, holding our breath and listening for any explosions.

Suddenly, there was a huge blast. The ground shuddered,

and the lights rattled and went out. In the darkness, Sulli screamed. I grabbed for Elga sitting next to me. The impact was close. We waited several long minutes for everything to still and the sirens to stop. When the lights came back on, we all back up the stairs.

It had been past midnight and pitch-dark when the sirens first sounded, and we had fled to the basement. Now, outlining the black-out curtains from the outside, we saw an eerie orange glow. We pulled a curtain back and saw the entire sky lit up as bright as day in the same orange light. The taillights of bombers blinked in the distance, but the sky remained strangely lit.

"What's happening?' Elga asked, her eyes wide open.

I was mesmerized as well. "How can this be?"

"They're flares," Father said. "The bombers drop them to see their targets. The flares have small parachutes attached. The heated air from the flares can keep the parachutes aloft for hours or even drive them upward."

"Wow!" Elga and I exclaimed in unison, transfixed by the phenomena.

All of a sudden, we were distracted by firetrucks barreling down the street. A massive fire was blazing in the direction of the train station. Something was ablaze.

The next day, we learned that a bomb had missed the station but made a direct hit on a house across the street. It was the home of a family known to the Rinnes. Less than a mile from us, the home was completely demolished. There were no survivors.

The Allies continued to target the railway and the refinery. With the recent bombings, the Rinnes proximity to the train station made it a dangerous place to live. The attacks also disrupted major supply lines to the city. There was less food and longer lines to get it. Life in Altenburg was becoming increasingly stressful.

Returning home from school a few days after the attempted train station bombing, Elga, Sulli, and I passed a crater in the center of the street. It was just a few blocks from the Rinnes. The hole was almost as wide as the street, which was now cordoned off by the army.

From neighbors standing nearby, we learned another bomb had been dropped but didn't explode. The unexploded shell had been defused and extracted just a few hours earlier. We ran to the house and met Father at the door as he was coming home from the refinery. Together, we all rushed inside.

"Is everyone alright?" Father exclaimed.

Mother, the color drained from her face, sat in a chair, still obviously shaken.

In a weak voice, she said, "Yes, thank God we're alright, but Hermanis, it was in the light of day, and there was no warning. The bomb could have just as easily fallen on top of us. Maija, Oma, Opa, and I were all here and felt the tremors from the impact!"

Father rushed over, putting his arms around her.

"My God! I don't even want to think about what might have happened had it exploded. It's is no longer safe to live here. We have to get out of the area."

Holding hands with Opa on the couch, Oma spoke up.

"Some people are renting rooms in the countryside."

Stepping back from Mother, Father looked at Oma and asked, "How do you know this?"

"I've talked to the neighbor lady. She was raised in Crispendorf an hour south of here and is returning there soon.

Villagers are taking in boarders from the city. They raise their own vegetables and livestock for food, too."

"Do you think there would be something for us?" Mother asked.

"From what the neighbor has said, I would think so," Oma replied.

Thinking out loud, Father said, "I could continue working while you moved there. At least I'd know you'd all be safe."

Mother picked up Maija, cradling her in her arms. "Yes, we must think of our safety, but what about you, Hermanis? It's not safe for you here either. You must come too!"

"I have the security of a job here and must continue earning an income for as long as I can," Father said.

"And what about school?" Elga asked.

We had just settled into a daily routine and were enjoying our friends and classes.

"Of course, you'll go," Father replied. "Right now, your safety is the primary concern. The family needs to get out of Altenburg."

It didn't take long for our move to be arranged. Oma's friend provided us with the names of two couples willing to take us into their homes. Mother, Maija, Elga, and I would stay with one couple and Oma and Opa with another couple nearby.

On the day of our departure, we all gathered outside the building to wait for Janis, Father's driver, who would take us to Crispendorf.

Mother spoke to Marianne, her voice faltering, "We can never thank you and Officer Rinne enough for rescuing us from our fates in Riga."

For her kindness and friendship, Mother presented

Marianne with several yards of heavy wool fabric from the crate shipped to us from Latvia.

With tears in her eyes, Marianne looked at Mother.

"Thank you. We were only returning a kindness. You nurtured me back to health and provided a home for Sulli while I was recuperating. It was the least we could do for you."

Mother was holding Maija on her hip. Marianne leaned in closer to pinch Maija's cheek. Then she looked up to smile at us and said, "You all take good care of this little one, alright?"

Elga turned to Sulli, "You've been such a good friend to Biruta and me. You're the best!"

Joining Elga to embrace Sulli, I said, "You have to come to see us. The train here goes directly to Crispendorf."

"I don't know," Sulli said, turning to her mother. "It's not so easy. We may be moving soon, too."

It was awful how war uprooted everyone and made our futures uncertain.

"You have to promise to write," I said, brushing away a tear. "For now, our Father can carry your letters when he comes to visit us."

Janis drove up the street and stopped in front of the building. We loaded our few belongings into the vehicle and waved good-bye to Sulli, the Rinnes, and Father. Sadness overcame me again as we left. Saying farewell to loved ones, no matter how often it happened, never got any easier and was becoming an all too familiar occurrence.

CHAPTER 10
Crispendorf | Spring 1945

By early February 1945, a German defeat appeared imminent. Three of the Allied leaders; British Prime Minister Churchill, Soviet Premier Stalin, and U.S. President F. D. Roosevelt, met on the Crimean Peninsula in Yalta to discuss Hitler's surrender and plans for Nazi post-war reparations. Germany would be divided into four zones to be managed by the Allies of France, Great Britain, the Soviet Union, and the United States. Stalin promised new elections in the Soviet-occupied countries of Eastern Europe but never complied. Roosevelt was in poor health and died two months after the Yalta conference. He was heavily criticized for granting the Soviets too many concessions. [7]

A s the car rolled into Crispendorf, we looked out to see a typical country village. Small, well-kept bungalows lined its narrow, packed earthen streets. Only a few hundred people lived here. Oma, Opa, Mother, Maija, Elga, and I met our new landlords, Hans and Greta Schmidt. They were a middle-aged couple with no children and rented their upstairs apartment for income.

As village farmers, the couple raised a few chickens and rabbits, along with a pig and a goat. A small vegetable garden was planted on a thin strip of land running alongside their house. Their two-story bungalow reminded me of Oma and Opa's house in Mezparks, except there was a small barn attached. The house and barn created an "L" shaped structure, and behind the building was an outhouse. Everything about the village and the Schmidt's home was simple, tidy, and quiet. It was a change from the bustle of Altenburg near the city train station and the ten of us living together at the Rinne flat. Of more importance, we were safe. There would be no reason to bomb such a sleepy little village.

Hans and Greta were kind-hearted people. From the start, they welcomed us as their guests. Hans was tall and broad-shouldered, walking with a slight limp. We never learned whether he had been injured in the war, or his condition prevented him from serving. He was a man of few words but offered to help us at our every need.

Greta, who was no taller than Elga and I, was rosy-cheeked and always smiling. She was at once enamored with nine-month-old Maija and offered to bring a cup of goat's milk for her. At first shy, Maija buried her face in Mother's shoulder, refusing the milk. With some coaxing, she finally accepted the cup and grinned back at Greta.

Greta led us upstairs and showed us where we would be staying. Oma and Opa remained downstairs, waiting to be taken to their lodgings later. Our apartment was modest and spartan. There were two tiny bedrooms and a common area that had a sink, a stove, and a wooden table and chairs. It would be our new home. It only took a few minutes to unpack our things.

As we descended the stairs to the main floor of the Schmidt home, Greta added helpfully, "Tomorrow, I'll show you the shops where you can get your basic staples and supplies."

With his eyes lowered, Hans shyly invited us to join them for dinner.

"After we've eaten, I'll take Oma and Opa to meet their landlords just down the road," he added.

Pleased to have such kind hosts, we settled into their front room to wait for dinner while Greta went to the kitchen.

A delicious aroma soon permeated the home, and my stomach growled. Cheerfully, Greta came from the kitchen announcing dinner would be served and invited us around their table.

"We don't always eat this well, but you provided an excuse for Hans to kill one of our fattest rabbits so that I could make a stew," she said. "I even saved a few potatoes and flour to make dumplings."

Throwing his shoulders back, Hans added, "There's rationing here, but I trade my rabbits for other goods in neighboring villages." Then he scurried into the kitchen to help Greta bring out the food as we seated ourselves.

Rabbit, I thought to myself. Even though Oma had raised them in Mezparks and prepared them on occasion, I didn't like to eat them. Elga and I, sitting on either side of Mother, looked at each other and made soft gagging noises. Oma and Opa frowned, and Mother gave us an icy stare. She pinched us under the table just before the couple returned from the kitchen carrying plates of steaming food.

Greta dished the food onto individual plates. Hans passed one to each of us. Despite my misgivings, the savory smells made my mouth water. I took a plate and hesitated before taking a bite. The tender meat, along with the potato dumplings and gravy, melted in my mouth. It was one of the best meals I had eaten in months and fought the urge to lick my plate clean.

With dinner completed, Hans carried Oma and Opa's belongings to their lodgings a few doors down. We later learned Oma and Opa didn't have it so well. Their landlords were an older, miserly couple who had lost two sons in the war. They were ill-tempered and resentful, giving Oma and Opa a shabby lean-to next to the chicken coop in their barn.

Oma had no patience for their behavior and later huffed, "We've all suffered, and I'm sorry for their loss. No matter what, there's no excuse to be mean. They won't even spare a grain of wheat for us and instead save it for their chickens."

Pulling us aside with a mischievous grin, Oma added, "I borrowed a cup of wheat the other day to make Opa and me some porridge."

We all laughed, but from then on, Mother, Elga, and I made a point to share our food with Oma and Opa.

❧

Elga and I were 15 now and didn't go back to school. Although high school in Altenburg had been challenging, we missed classes and being with our new friends. In Crispendorf, schooling after the elementary grades wasn't provided.

Tending the Schmidt's garden plot and minding the chickens and rabbits became our full-time job. For our efforts, Hans and Greta shared a portion of their produce. As food shortages continued to escalate, Elga and I walked with Mother or Oma to a neighboring village to trade vegetables and eggs for basic staples like flour, salt, or imitation coffee.

Mother befriended a butcher in the town a few miles away. Elga and I often accompanied her to his shop to get discards from his sausage making. She would make a broth from the scraps, adding dandelion greens to make a tasty soup. One day, feeling confident that the area was safe and we could handle the task alone, Mother sent Elga and me on an errand to see the butcher.

Arriving at his shop, the butcher recognized us and waved us in. Elga and I chatted with him, watching as he wrapped a soup bone in paper. All at once, we heard a disturbance in the street. The butcher came out from behind his counter, and we joined him to go to the storefront window.

A crowd of villagers was lining the street. They were watching German soldiers with dogs and rifles marching a group of emaciated bodies through the center of town right in front of the shop. There were over two dozen souls with hollowed-out frames making it difficult to determine whether they were men or women or both. They were just skin and bone, moving skeletons really, scarcely able to pick up their feet as they trudged along. The parade shuffled along in dirty, tattered rags that appeared to have once been striped uniforms. I squeezed my eyes shut, trying to make the awful scene disappear.

"Who are they?" Elga whispered, asking the butcher.

The butcher hesitated, "I'm not sure. I've heard rumors about Nazi political prisons, but I didn't know they actually existed. Or perhaps they are criminals or prisoners of war."

Some prisoners begged the villagers for water. When water was given, the soldiers took it from them and drank it themselves or gave it to their dogs. Other soldiers kicked the containers of water out of inmates' hands, leaving them to lick the few drops that spilled on their hands and fingers. Elga and I were drawn to the terror as we stood behind the safety of the storefront glass.

Whoever they were, from the pained and hopeless expressions on their faces, it was apparent they were suffering as they staggered along. Some stumbled and fell to the ground. When they did, the soldiers prodded them with rifles to get up. Those who couldn't walk were picked up by their comrades. They were dragged along the dusty road so as not to be left behind. We stood in shocked silence as the miserable parade continued through the town.

"Those damn Nazis," the butcher said, shaking his head. "I'm sorry, but no one deserves to be treated that way."

Dazed, we watched as the spectacle drifted down the road and out of sight. After they were gone, we were speechless for several minutes before moving back to the counter. Elga and I timidly took the butcher's small bundle and thanked him as we left.

Needing to make one more stop in the village, Elga and I completed our task and made our way to the road that would lead us back home. Still numbed by what we had seen, we walked along in silence. We slowed our pace and began picking dandelion leaves in the ditches. In the early springtime breezes, a few birds chirped in the trees, but their songs did little to improve our mood.

Then suddenly, Bang! Bang! Bang! And then another Bang! Bang! Bang! Gunshots rang out in the distance. Jumping back onto the road and creeping forward, we turned our heads side-to-side, scanning the area around us. We walked this way for another half mile. Then Elga stopped in her tracks, putting her hand over her mouth.

"What is it, Elga?" I whispered.

She didn't say anything but raised her arm and pointed her finger in front of her. Following her gaze, 30 yards ahead, I could see a half a dozen bloodied bodies lying in a grassy area not far from the road. Even from a distance, I recognized the gray, ragged prison uniforms. Apparently unable to keep up, some of the prisoners had been shot.

Elga and I didn't move a muscle. We knew we had to walk past the bodies to get home.

"What are we going to do?" I whispered.

Without hesitation, Elga shouted, "Run!"

Staring straight ahead, we ran as fast as we could past the corpses until we reached home. We bolted up the stairs two at a time to Mother.

Seeing the terror in our eyes, Mother rushed to us, "What happened?"

"Soldiers were marching a group of prisoners through the village! They were skin and bones and could hardly walk!" Elga blurted out, panting so hard she could hardly speak.

"On the way home, we heard shots. Then, we saw dead bodies and had to run past them to get home!" I choked on each word as I held back the urge to scream.

"How horrible! I should've never let you go to the village alone!" Mother cried out, wrapping her arms around us. Still, her words and actions provided little comfort to the horrors we had seen.

After that day, Mother didn't let us go to the village alone again. The specter of those bodies haunted my nightmares that evening and for many nights to come. The ghastly images are still etched in my memory.

꩜

By early April, we were surprised to hear radio broadcasts announcing Hitler was losing the war. Despite the news, people in the village refused to believe the reports. Rumors spread that Hitler held a secret weapon, ensuring a decisive Nazi victory.

In the last days of April 1945, the Soviet army approached Berlin. Later, news reports confirmed that when they were surrounded, Hitler and many of his top aides had hidden in an underground bunker and committed suicide by taking cyanide capsules.

Hitler's successor, Admiral Donitz, officially surrendered to the Allies on May 7, 1945. A day later, on May 8th, the whole of Europe celebrated V.E. Day, victory day in Europe. Six years of war were finally over.

In the days and weeks following the end of the war, Nazi death camps were discovered across Germany, exposing the horrors of Hitler's atrocities toward the Jews. Only then did I better understand the awful scene Elga and I had witnessed just a few weeks earlier.

After the war was declared over, hundreds of thousands of refugees who had fled their homelands, as we had, were scattered across Europe and Germany. Our family was waiting to hear when the Soviets would be leaving Latvia. With our country's independence restored, we would return home. Until then, our family remained in Crispendorf.

❧

One morning when Elga and I went down to collect eggs from the hens, we heard a rumbling in the distance roaring closer and closer.

"Biruta, what is that sound?" Elga said, stopping to listen.

"I'm not sure, but let's get in the house," I said, my heart racing as I grabbed the eggs.

We ran upstairs to Mother and Maija. I hurried to place the eggs in a bowl on the table for later. Mother, who had also heard the thundering noise, was glad we had come inside. We went to the window to look toward the direction of the clamor.

In the distance, we saw a cloud of dust and military tanks approaching Crispendorf. That they were coming here, concerned us. The tension only mounted as they arrived in the village. American soldiers went from house-to-house with their guns drawn, searching each building. We stood motionless by the window, not knowing what to do. We saw a neighbor race across the yard toward our house and herard her rap loudly on the door.

"Stay here with Maija," Mother directed Elga and me. "I'll see what the neighbor knows."

Flying down the stairs, Mother returned a few minutes later.

"She said the soldiers are looking for any German troops who may be hiding among us. They are checking identification papers for each person in each household." Seeing the concern on our faces, Mother added, "Our papers are in order, and we have nothing to fear. Everything is alright, and they'll soon be gone."

I knew we weren't hiding any German soldiers, but I tensed at the thought of our family being questioned. Would the American soldiers wonder why Latvians were living in a German household? In the war, the Americans and Soviets were Allies. Would they know we fled Latvia to escape the Soviets?

I saw the soldiers enter the house next door, and my anxiety grew. Suddenly, I felt the urge to use the toilet. The presence of the soldiers had caused such a commotion that no one noticed as I crept down the stairs to slip out the back door and head for the outhouse.

When I finished, I cracked the door open and heard soldiers already inside the house. Frightened to go back, I eased the door shut and stayed inside the outhouse. Soon, I heard Mother and Elga outside calling out my name, looking for me. Through a crack in the door, I could see the search spill out into the yard with the soldiers assisting them. I didn't know what to do, but I knew I had created a disturbance — seconds ticked by as I summoned my courage. Slowly, I eased the outhouse door open and red-faced stepped out.

Everyone turned to look my way. For a moment, no one said anything. Seeing I was safe, Elga and Mother burst out laughing. The tension in the air broke and for a few minutes, I was the source of everyone's amusement. Even the soldiers, who needed to go on to the next house, left snickering.

"Biruta, didn't you hear us calling?" Elga asked.

"We were worried something might have happened to you!" Mother exclaimed.

Profoundly embarrassed, I said nothing. As we went inside, Mother and Elga began to giggle and tease me again. I stomped up the stairs, my stomach growling. It had been a dramatic morning, and I hadn't even eaten breakfast yet. Then I noticed the bowl of eggs I had collected that morning sitting empty on the table. Adding insult to my injury, the soldiers had taken them. Although I hadn't been snatched away as Mother and Elga had feared, the eggs were gone.

It was a time of great chaos, and things were changing daily. With the war over and the Soviets still in the Baltics, the situation remained unresolved. While everyone waited for conditions in Europe to stabilize, Father continued to stay with the Rinnes in Altenburg to earn money for our pending return to Latvia.

Unexpectedly, the oil refinery where Father worked was taken over by the Allies as a part of Germany's war reparations. As a result, Father lost his job. Word spread that the Soviets would be in charge of the assets in Altenburg. The Rinne women, fearful of their direct connection to a German officer, made arrangements to leave their flat and take temporary shelter further west with relatives. Father was suddenly out of a job and homeless. He made plans to join us in Crispendorf.

We welcomed Father back with open arms. Our family, now reunited, went upstairs to our apartment, and he told us about the situation in Altenburg. We were happy to be together again, but the uncertainty about our future clouded our reunion.

In a quiet moment, Mother asked Father, "When do you think we'll be able to go back to Latvia?"

"I'm not sure. The whole of Europe is upside down right now," he said. "We'll just have to wait until everything sorts itself out."

Suddenly, I thought about Sulli, her mother, and grandmother and worried about her brother and father, both in the German army.

"Where will Sulli, her mother, and grandmother go? And what about Sulli's brother and Officer Rinne?" I asked.

"I'm afraid the end of the war has brought hardship and uncertainty to them as well," he answered. "Sulli, her mother, and grandmother are going to live with a cousin in the western part of Germany. They are leaving, as we did, with only the things they can carry."

Father hesitated, shaking his head and taking a deep breath before he continued, "They will need each other's support right now. I'm sorry to tell you, but shortly after you left Altenburg, Officer Rinne went missing in action. He was on a supply train that was bombed. There were survivors, but he has not been heard from since and is presumed dead."

Elga and I gasped, and Mother's hand flew up to her throat.

Father continued, "Sulli's mother and brother are trying to get additional information from the German military authorities, but they have heard nothing more."

A deep sadness came over me. I recalled not so long ago when Elga, Sulli, and I had talked about our fathers and how we worried about them during their absences. Father was here now, but I ached for Sulli and her family. They would have to go on now without the certainty of knowing what had happened to Officer Rinne.

Sulli adored her father, and now I was helpless to console her. A tear rolled down my cheek, and I cried softly, recalling how Officer Rinne had made it possible for our family to leave Latvia. Now all I could do was say a silent prayer for Sulli, her family, and her father.

❧

In June, there was no more clarity about our family's future. We heard world news over the radio, but regional news about the situation in Germany was posted in bulletins at the village center. Father went there daily to read them, returning to share what he had learned.

"It's maddening," Father said after a return from the village one day. "The reports say the Allies are encouraging refugees to return to their homelands. They don't understand with the Communists occupying our countries, we don't want to go back. They don't know or aren't acknowledging Stalin's atrocities in the Baltics."

After a trip to the village center, Father usually stopped to visit with our landlords before coming upstairs. Today, he raced up the steps two at a time to our living quarters, slamming the door shut. I frowned at Elga. It was not like Father. Something was wrong.

"Stalin has been given control of the Baltics with promises of free elections!" Father shouted.

"Oh, no!" Mother exclaimed, reaching out to grab Father's arm. "Free elections! Do the Allies actually believe that? If Stalin is in charge, we'll never be able to return to Latvia!"

"It's even worse than that. The Allies are dividing Germany into four post-war zones: American; British; French; and Soviet. The whole region of Thrungren, where we are right now, is in the Eastern zone. It is to be taken over by the Soviets!" Father said, crumpling onto the chair to hold his head in his hands. "I can't believe it! We risked everything to come here and can't go home," he groaned. "Now, we're in the very zone designated for the Russians."

Hearing the news, I felt sick to my stomach.

Grasping the consequences of what Father was saying, Mother rasped in a barely audible voice, "If we can't go home, and we can't stay here, where will we go?"

Father looked at her. "There is one hope. After hearing the

news, a Latvian representative is going to talk to the Americans. He's advocating for the refugees here to be transferred to the American zone."

A few days passed, and we heard nothing. Then early one morning without notice, several jeeps with American soldiers appeared in Crispendorf and went door-to-door, talking to refugees.

The United Nations Relief and Rehabilitation Administration (UNRRA) had set up over 300 Displaced Person's camps, or DP camps, throughout the western region of Germany. The closest to Cripsendorf was Camp Fischbach in the American zone. It was about 200 miles west in the village of Fischbach outside of Nuremberg. It was set up to accommodate about 1,500 refugees.

The U.S. Army would provide transportation from East Germany to the American zone if we chose to go. However, we needed to pack and be ready to leave by morning. It would be our only opportunity to be transferred before the Soviets took over the region. My parents readily agreed to go.

It was all so sudden. As the soldiers left, a sadness filled me, realizing we would not be returning to Riga. However, there was also relief in knowing we had somewhere to go removed from Stalin's oppression.

Immediately after the soldiers left, Father and Mother went to inform Oma and Opa about the sudden change in circumstances. Elga and I went with them. When Oma heard the plan, her shoulders drooped, and she wrung her hands.

"A DP camp? But Opa and I had planned to return to our home in Mezparks. We're too old for such an undertaking. I'm afraid we'd be a burden to the family."

"Nonsense," Father told them. "We've come this far

together. There'll be no abandoning anyone now. You know what Latvia was like under Soviet occupation. It would be dangerous for you to return, and you certainly can't stay here," he said, glancing around at their surroundings.

"You're family," Mother said with tenderness to her parents. "We have every intention of taking care of you, just as you have always taken care of us."

Elga and I smiled at each other pleased to hear our parents confirm their commitment to Oma and Opa and glad when they agreed to come with us.

Janis Bremanis, Father's friend and driver, had also contacted him. With the turmoil and news that the Soviets would be taking over Altenburg and the Eastern portion of Germany, they agreed it was better to face uncertainty with friends than to face it alone. Janis and his wife, Aina, drove their car with their possessions and their prized instruments – her harp and his violin – from Altenburg to Crispendorf. From here on out, the Bremanis planned to follow our family.

The rest of the day, our family hastily threw our belongings together. What didn't fit into our suitcases was bundled into sheets or blankets. I went to bed that evening, with thoughts of the American zone racing through my head. I wondered what a DP camp was like and how long we would have to stay. Maybe we would even get to go to America someday.

The next morning, the whole family was up before the sun rose on the eastern horizon. A song thrush chirped its greeting to the day, reflecting our hopes for a new beginning.

Hans and Father brought over Oma and Opa's bundles, and Oma's replenished milk can with foods for Maija, now a year old. Oma and Opa followed them to wait with our family. Mother, distracted by their arrival, turned around to see Maija pulling random items from a bundle that had just been secured and mildly scolded her. Oma sat with their possessions, singing a familiar hymn while Opa hummed along. Father greeted Janis and Aina, who had just arrived in their car. We all waited together for the soldiers to arrive.

When the army trucks appeared, the soldiers jumped out and called for us to load up. It was time to go. We hugged Hans and Greta goodbye, thanking them for all they had done for us. We loaded our belongings onto the back of an open-aired truck and got in to sit on long wooden benches. The truck would take us to the train station, and from there, the train would take us to Camp Fischbach. Sitting next to each other, Elga and I smiled and playfully nudged each other with our shoulders. We were going to the American zone.

The truck rumbled down the road, and the Bremanis' vehicle fell in behind and followed it. The truck made more stops to pick up additional refugees, so the Bremanis drove their car ahead to the train station. When we arrived, Janis was arguing with the soldier in charge. The authorities were insisting that his vehicle was a war reparation and couldn't be taken to the American zone. It would need to be surrendered. Janis was visibly upset but eventually gave in, grudgingly unloading their articles from the car.

Having overheard part of Janis' argument with the soldier dampened some of my enthusiasm about the Americans. Stepping off the truck and looking around the railyard, more apprehension set in. No passenger train was in sight. Instead, next to the station was a single-engine train with a long line of empty wooden boxcars idling on the tracks. I looked at Father and pointed at the freight cars.

"Is that how we're getting to the American zone?"

Gazing at the train, Father stated flatly, "I believe it is."

Oma overheard our conversation and, as usual, tried to remain upbeat.

"It's not a long way and shouldn't take more than half a day," she said, playing down our concern.

"We can endure," Mother added. "It can't be that bad."

Elga, out of Mother's and Oma's line of sight, rolled her eyes.

"Hmm, I'm not so sure," she whispered to me.

Soon the station became a flurry of activity as other truckloads of families arrived. Our family and the Bremanis, along with other refugees, were assigned to boxcars about 20 people per car. We loaded our belongings and boarded. The freight cars were worn but clean. Racks of pallets lined the inside walls to stretch out and rest. Fresh bales of hay provided places to sit during the journey. Even with our bundles, there was plenty of space to sit, lie down, or move around.

When all the passengers had boarded, the train whistle blew a long plaintive whine. The rail car doors closed, and the train brakes hissed their release. The pistons began their slow churn, and the train lurched ahead, chugging away slowly and then picking up speed.

After a few minutes of getting accustomed to the rhythm and motion of the train, people began to relax, arranging their bundles and bales for lounging or napping. I sighed with relief as the train got underway, and we clicked faster and faster on the rails. It wasn't the most comfortable way to travel, but people were chattering and laughing, glad to be leaving the Eastern zone.

Several minutes into the journey, Janis stood up and walked over to the rail car door. He cracked it open for some fresh air and looked outside. Sliding the door open wider to get a better view, he looked at the countryside gliding by and then toward the sun in the sky. He turned back around with his brows furrowed and nostrils flared. Pounding his fist on the side of the boxcar, he shouted unintelligibly. At first, I couldn't understand what Janis was saying, but then I heard him clearly.

"We're heading east toward the rising sun! We're going in the wrong direction!"

Alarmed, people stood up, moving toward the door to see for themselves. Others confirmed it, and an uproar erupted from the passengers. The engine was several cars ahead, and there was no way to reach the engineer. With no recourse, people angrily sat down and continued grumbling.

My heart was pounding. "Father! What'll we do?"

"There's nothing we can do until the train stops," Father spat out, pounding a fist into his other hand.

It wasn't long before the train slowed for the next station. When it screeched to a halt, Father, Janis, and several men jumped out of the train car, running toward the front of the train. They pounded on boxcars along the way, alerting others to the problem. More men jumped out and joined them as they ran to speak to the engineer.

Women and children waited in the rail compartments, nerves on edge. Some wrung their hands as they sat while others paced. Tension filled the air inside the boxcar. What would happen to us if we ended up further east, deeper into the Soviet zone?

As the train idled, the pistons beat out a slow rhythm, and I watched billowing puffs of steam rise into the clear blue sky. All we could do was wait until the men came back. It seemed like hours before they returned.

Father, Janis, and the men climbed back into the freight

car. Everyone clustered around them to hear the news. Mother grabbed Father's arm and riveted her eyes into him, pressing him.

"What did you find out?"

"We confronted the engineer," Father said, his voice rising so all could hear. "He feigned ignorance. I think he thought no one would notice. The engineer is German. I'm sure he isn't pleased the Allies are taking over his country. He said he thought his orders were to take us east but suggested he could be persuaded otherwise."

Mother's eyes widened, "What did you do?"

"We did the only thing we could do. Between us, we took up a collection of silver and German marks to pay him off. He knew we wanted to go to the American zone and saw an opportunity to take advantage of us. Thank goodness, Janis noticed our direction," Father said, slapping him on the back, "and the engineer took our money."

Wiping his brow on his sleeve and sitting down on a bale, Father took a deep breath and continued, "Now, we wait for the engineer to turn the train around. We're fortunate there's a 'wye' junction at this station. The engineer can reverse the train onto a parallel track to take us in the opposite direction. We've lost some time and money, but the money will be well worth it to get out of the Soviet zone."

It was late afternoon by the time the train started heading in the right direction. The sun was beginning its slow arc toward the west. Besides the engineer's "error", the train made frequent stops along the way, significantly delaying our travel.

While stopping at stations, we got off the train to stretch our legs or to take toilet breaks. Occasionally, there were Red Cross volunteers handing out sandwiches and soups. Other times the train stopped on the tracks allowing other trains to pass. Staples such as oil, coal, grain, and foodstuffs to be taken to the cities took priority over us.

At twilight, the skyline turned several shades of pink and purple before darkness settled in. The train stopped for the evening in the middle of a large field. We were taken aback. No one had expected an overnight stay. After a long day of travel, people were tired and irritable, complaining of hunger. A sandwich eaten several hours ago couldn't stifle our stomachs, growling in rebellion.

Suddenly, someone shouted, "Look! There are potato plants in the fields! Maybe there are potatoes for us to eat!"

The observation caused people to jump from the train and run into the fields to begin digging. We joined in, and piles of potatoes were gathered. Overjoyed, people searched in a nearby grove of trees to find branches. Soon small fires glowed in the field, and potatoes roasted until they were soft. When they cooled, we devoured them.

The stars began to twinkle in the evening sky, my stomach was full, and my eyelids drooped. I staggered back into our boxcar, falling asleep on a pallet. The next morning, only the jolt from the train moving forward to resume our journey woke me.

Mid-morning, the train stopped at a station where coffee, soups, and rye bread were distributed. I was glad Oma had thought to bring along some white bread for Maija. The coarse rye bread and coffee weren't suitable for her. Mother was grateful, too, that at the stations, milk was provided for the children. Throughout the day, the train continued to make frequent stops. Elga and I took turns singing songs and playing with Maija to keep her and us occupied. Still, the hours dragged on.

"Oma," Elga said, "I thought you said this trip was only going to take a half-day."

"Well, I had no idea we'd have to turn around or be making so many stops!" Oma huffed. She and Opa shifted uncomfortably on one of the bales, looking very worn and tired.

The rest of the day passed. Finally, just before midnight on June 23, 1945, we arrived at the Fischbach train station in the American zone. It was St. John's Eve, Latvia's traditional celebration of midsummer's night. No one was in the mood to celebrate. Exhaustion from the two-day trip registered on everyone's faces.

The train came to a halt, and the boxcar doors opened. We were told to leave our belongings on the train to be retrieved in the morning. In a tired stupor, we climbed onto the backs of army trucks to be taken to Camp Fischbach to be processed into the camp by the United Nations Relief and Rehabilitation Administration (UNRRA). They and the U.S. Army would be taking care of us now.

CHAPTER 11
UNRRA & The U.S. Army

Following the Victory in Europe (VE Day) in May 1945, 6 million displaced persons remained in the Western zone of Germany, with an additional 6-7 million in the Soviet Occupied zone. In the months immediately following, an estimated 7 million people returned to their homeland... However, by September 1945, approximately 1.2 million people remained in Western Germany.

At the time the United Nations did not exist and the United Nations Relief and Rehabilitation Administration (UNRRA) was established when 44 nations agreed to join an international organization to provide care for those left in Germany.

The UNRRA and the International Refugee Organization (IRO) were established as temporary agencies to provide post-war relief care and rehabilitation as well as repatriation and resettlement of people displaced by the events of World War II.

While UNRRA's ultimate objective was repatriation, within the camps relief expanded to include... providing food, clothes, health care and accommodation, as well as ... child welfare, ...education, ...and employment opportunities.[8]

T he gates of Camp Fischbach were only a short distance from the train station. Passing through them, we stopped in front of a long, wooden one story building lit outside by one dim bulb. A half dozen staff members were waiting to greet us in front of the building. Upon exiting the truck, Father gave our family names to UNRRA personnel who checked us off on their lists. We were assigned a building and handed bed sacks of straw for sleeping. Carrying them, we followed a staff member to our lodgings.

On a dark, moonless night heavy with clouds, we walked a short distance on a gravel road. Only an occasional streetlight broke the darkness, casting eerie circular shadows on the ground. I rubbed my eyes, but I could see little. Unable to clearly make out our surroundings, I had no sense for the size of the camp.

In no time, we were in front of a barrack, and the staff member led us inside. It was one large open space with dozens of two and three-tiered bunk beds. Perhaps because Maija was with us, our family was given a corner partitioned off with a wall. Oma and Opa were directed to beds in the open section. Utterly exhausted, I didn't care about our sleeping arrangements. I threw my bed sack onto a lower bunk, plopped down upon it, and fell asleep.

The next day, I woke up to bright sunlight filtering through the dirty windows. I guessed it was already mid-morning. I flung my arms over my head and lengthened the muscles in my arms and legs for one long stretch. Brushing the sleep from my eyes, I peeked around the divider into the adjoining room. It hadn't been a dream. It was a barrack with rows and rows of bunks in one large room. At least 60 other people were lodged with us. Later, someone said the camp had once housed draftees for the German Army. It indeed looked to be the case.

As I looked around the area, the barrack wasn't just dirty. It was filthy. A thick coat of grime coated everything. Mouse droppings, dead insects, and food encrusted plates and utensils littered the floor. People milled about in a daze, wondering what to tackle first to make the conditions bearable. Oma and Opa were sitting on their lower bunks, conversing with some refugees around them. Sandwiched between a row of beds with just a few feet of space between them, they had even less room than we did.

I ducked my head back around the partition and examined our space more closely. Our small corner only accommodated two sets of bunk beds with a narrow table squeezed between them. Maija's basket, which she had long outgrown for sleeping, sat on top of the table filled with articles of her clothing. She had slept with Mother during the night.

I heard Elga stir in the bed above me. Father and Mother were sitting across from me on the lower bunk. They had gotten our things from the train and were stowing them beneath the beds.

I watched for a few minutes before I said to them, "We aren't really staying here, are we?"

Father stopped what he was doing to look up at me and said, "I'm afraid so."

"In this crusty old barrack? It's a dump."

"For the time being, we will have to make do," Mother said. "At least we haven't been hauled off by the Soviets to some godforsaken place."

Gazing around the cramped area, I wasn't sure we were much better off.

Oma had walked over to join our family and overheard the end of our conversation. She smiled and said, "This can be our new adventure."

Hearing us talk, Elga looked down from her bunk. She scowled as she got her first good look at our surroundings.

"That's a little farfetched, isn't it, Oma?"

Mother, smiling weakly, tried to distract Elga and me, holding out a small loaf of bread.

"Are you grumpy girls hungry?" she teased. "I saved it from this morning. I'm afraid it's all we have for breakfast."

We hadn't eaten since our last train stop, and we were famished.

"Is this all?" I asked, thinking that calling it "breakfast" was clearly a misnomer.

Elga climbed down from her bunk and sat with me on my bed while we wolfed it down, topping it off with some water. Unsatisfied, I longed for the roasted potatoes we had two evenings ago.

Jumping up and smoothing out her rumpled clothes, Elga asked, "Can Biruta and I go outside to check out the camp?"

"Yes, but don't take too long," Mother replied. "We've set up a cleaning committee and will be starting soon. Heaven knows, we have a lot of work to do," as she dragged a finger across the dirty tabletop between the beds.

Elga and I slipped on our shoes and headed for the door. We walked outside and scanned the immediate area. Our building was one of four identical wooden clapboard barracks sitting next to each other on one large section of land. The buildings sat on hard-packed earth with scrawny tufts of grass sporadically pushing their way to the surface between them. Across the road, we saw another section with four additional barracks.

We strolled north toward the center of camp on a road between the two sections. Further up, another road running east and west crossed our path, dividing the camp into quadrants. The main gate, where we had entered last night, was on the west and beyond the entrance, a forest. To the east, a small lot attached to the eastern border of camp held a one-story L-shaped building with a sign labeled "Ambulance and Hospital" hanging on the front. Past the hospital, were railroad tracks and the Fischbach train station where we had arrived last evening. Behind the station were fields of tall yellow grasses.

Beyond the dividing road were another two large sections, each with four additional barracks. North of them was a large open field. There were a total of 16 barracks bordering the camp, eight on the north border, and eight on the south. Four or five more barracks were at the center of the camp, along with a church and buildings labeled UNRRA and the U.S. Army administration offices. Among them were various other buildings and duplexes.

A few American soldiers patrolled the area and nodded to us as we passed. Later, we learned the soldiers were meant to keep intruders out. On occasion, hungry locals tried to break into camp because food rations were stockpiled here. Over time, tensions eased and the soldiers took chocolate bars to the village children and oranges to the pretty girls.

Elga and I went to investigate the buildings at the center of camp. One building had a sign hanging outside the entrance designating separate hours for men and women. Curious, we peeked inside. It was a large open room with rows of showerheads along each of its four walls. Sloping floors led to a drain at its center. There wasn't much privacy here, I thought and grimaced.

Next to the shower building was another barrack with sinks hung on the outside walls. Inside were pit toilets with a wall dividing the room in half, designating one side for women, the other side for men.

"Oh, great," Elga said, her words filled with sarcasm. "This looks just like home."

Dragging our heels, we shuffled back to our barrack in silence. Living here would be quite an adjustment.

We saw other individuals inspecting the surroundings and politely nodded. Besides Latvian, Polish greetings were returned. Soon realizing our exploration had taken us away from the family for some time, we stepped up our pace. We didn't want to keep Mother waiting. When we got back, the barrack was a beehive of activity.

"There you two are," Mother said. "I was starting to get worried. We have cleaning supplies from the Army, and everyone is working to scrub down every item and inch of the barrack."

Men carried bunk beds and furniture outside to wipe them down and tightened bolts to sturdy them. Women scrubbed the floor on hands and knees, while others washed doors, walls, and windows. Older children swept and dusted. Feeling guilty that we had stayed away too long, Elga and I asked Mother what we could do.

"Oma and Opa are outside on the other side of the building," she said. "They are washing the metal plates and utensils found on the floor and boiling them over a fire to sanitize them. I'm sure they could use some help. At least you could lend a hand keeping an eye on Maija."

"Plates and utensils?" Elga asked. "How do we prepare meals here?"

"There's hardly room to sit down to eat," I added.

"For now, the Army will be bringing a hot meal at lunchtime to the barracks. Later, there'll be a centralized kitchen. Now go help Oma and Opa," Mother said, snapping a wet rag to shoo us along.

In the beginning, we were only served bread in the morning and evenings. At noon, the Army dropped off a large metal drum of hot soup, placing it outside between two barracks. Standing in line to ladle a portion into our newly cleaned bowls, we usually had a tasteless pea soup and called it "the green terror". After numerous complaints, a greasy beef and macaroni soup alternated with the pea soup for our lunch.

One day, I entered our barrack and saw Elga reading alone in our section. The rest of the family had gone for a walk to visit the Bremanis living elsewhere in the camp. A large gallon jug containing a red substance sat on the small table between the bunks. I looked around, and throughout the room, saw similar jars distributed to each family.

"What...in the world...is that?" I asked Elga staring at the jug.

"I'm not sure. The Army handed them out this morning. Mother said it's made from tomatoes for added nutrition. It's supposed to add flavor to our food."

"What food?" I asked. "All we get is bread and those horrid soups."

"Maybe it's for the bread," Elga said, shrugging her shoulders. "I think it's called ketchup."

"Well, I'm hungry. There's extra bread from breakfast, right? Should we try some?"

Elga and I dug through a small crate where the family kept our eating utensils and found a knife. Grabbing the bread and opening the jar, we spread the strange red substance on a slice. I looked at Elga, daring her.

"You go first."

She took a bite, and her eyes lit up.

"Not bad," she announced. "Better than those nasty old soups."

I tried some and nodded in agreement. From then on, for us, ketchup sandwiches replaced "the green terror".

Later, other shipments of food arrived. Cans of luncheon meat, peanut butter, and chocolate bars made it a red-letter day. However, it was the instant coffee and cigarettes that proved to be the most valuable. The cigarettes were as precious as gold in the village. We traded them for fresh vegetables and eggs, which supplemented our meals.

Clothing and household goods were also provided. Whenever an UNRRA truck came into camp, anyone seeing it alerted the others. A crowd formed around the truck wherever it stopped to unload its shipment.

"Oh, look! Large boxes. It's got to be something good," Oma said as we joined a group surrounding a newly arrived truck.

Staff started opening boxes, pulling out bundles, and throwing them out into the crowd.

The first woman grabbing a bundle examined it and held it over her head, doing a lively jig.

"Sheets!" she shouted.

Cheers arose as others grabbed to get their allotment.

"Praise the Lord!" Oma shouted. "Now we can cover those wretched straw mattresses. I'm tired of waking up every morning with itchy welts."

Later, heavier blankets arrived for the colder winter months. A few weeks later, another shipment of blankets came, creating a surplus. Not letting anything go to waste, Oma and her friends devised a use for them. The extra blankets were hung as "walls" in the barracks to partition off areas for each family.

Clothing shipments also came in bulk. Typically, they were military surplus in the same style and color of drab khaki or olive green. Even so, Elga and I tore through the boxes to find something new to wear. Giggling, we put on some recent donations and completed our look with Army boots, the only shoes provided. Running to see our friends, we all pranced around the barracks laughing at our identical uniforms. There would be no style competitions in camp.

Another day, while Elga and I were lingering outside the

barrack, Mother called to us. Assuming she had an errand or wanted us to watch Maija, we hurried inside.

"I have a surprise for you," she said as we entered.

Glancing at each other, we wondered what Mother had in store for us. From behind her back, she pulled out two pairs of slacks, both in rich shades of gray.

"Where did you get these?" Elga exclaimed.

"No one in camp has anything like this!" I added.

"Some light-weight flannel blankets arrived a few days ago. I grabbed some and stitched these myself," Mother explained. "I thought you might enjoy wearing something different from everyone else."

Mother's awareness touched me deeply. She was clearly sensitive to our bumpy transition to camp life. Elga and I thanked her. We rushed to put on our new slacks and went to show our friends.

❧

Many children and young people were at Camp Fischbach. Schooling had been disrupted for us as we fled Latvia with our families. In the fall, several Latvian university professors and teachers in camp organized a school for both the upper and lower grades. Many were high-level instructors accomplished in their fields. We were provided excellent teachers, allowing us to continue our educations. Even students from smaller refugee camps nearby and from as far away as Munich came here to attend school.

Elga's and my interrupted second year of high school resumed. Our class consisted of around 20 students. Although our class size was small, no space was available for a classroom. Classes were held outdoors in the fields or under the trees.

When cold weather came, we crowded into a barrack with the younger students to study.

My day was long and began at sunrise. Refugees gathered at the center of the camp for the raising of the American, Latvian, and Polish flags. There were announcements of world and local events and camp activities. Afterward, I hurried to school early to tutor with a teacher who had been an architect. I had always dreamed of being one and hoped the extra instruction would aid me in pursuing the career.

In our classes, the teachers worked us rigorously. There were few schoolbooks, making it even more challenging. Usually, we were assigned pen and paper tasks of lengthy essays and complicated math problems.

At the end of the school day, despite the lack of facilities or equipment, physical education was required. Mostly, we ran cross country track through the forest bordering the camp's perimeter. Later, some gym equipment arrived and was installed in the adjacent field north of the camp. The girls enjoyed performing team formations on the parallel bars while the boys worked on other apparatus for strength training. Homework took up my evenings. The days sped by, leaving me little free time.

For entertainment, the adults in the camp organized social and cultural activities. Latvian books brought out of the country were read and reviewed in literary groups. A Latvian minister and a priest led weekly church services and religious discussions. Choral and folk dance groups for all ages, reinforced our traditions. Plans were already in progress for a Latvian Song Festival. Despite the war and our displacement, every effort was made to keep our culture alive.

At Camp Fischbach, UNRRA and the U.S. Army had done much to make us feel comfortable in our temporary surroundings. Yet displacement and post-war shortages kept us dependent on both organizations for food, clothing, and shelter. Our lives had been upended and put on hold. We had no real sense of belonging. This communal camp living wasn't natural. I hated it and wanted to get on with my life.

CHAPTER 12

Camp Fischbach

UNRRA was conceived as a short-term organization to deal with an emergency; however, as the full level of displacement and destruction in Europe became evident, it was apparent that facilities [i.e., DP camps] would have to become more longstanding than first imagined. By 1946, Germany was also dealing with an influx of refugees who were fleeing what were then Soviet-controlled states. It was becoming clear that UNRRA's goal of complete or near complete repatriation would not be accomplished, and resettlement became the priority.[9]

I n January 1946, Elga and I turned 16 years old. Our family had been living at Camp Fischbach for seven months. Living in a DP camp made me appreciate all we had left behind in Riga. I longed for friends and relatives that I might never see again. I missed our grandparents' home in Mezparks and the joy it provided. I tolerated life at camp because there was no alternative. I kept my spirits up by focusing on school, family, and friends. Our family's future was unclear, but I was still young and dreamed of a life beyond Camp Fischbach.

I was concerned for Father and Mother. Both in their forties, their promising careers as physicians were interrupted as we fled the Soviet re-occupation of Latvia. The war made it difficult, if not impossible, for them to keep up with medical advances. Although Father had worked in Altenburg, Mother hadn't worked as a physician since we left Riga almost two years ago. Then an opportunity presented itself to Father.

"Elsa, I've been approached by the camp administrator," Father beamed. "They need doctors at the camp hospital. The supplies and equipment are outdated and limited, and we'd be donating our services. Still, we'd be able to keep up with our skills as physicians."

Mother's face lit up, "That's wonderful news! I always wanted to practice medicine again."

They both began working at the hospital shortly after.

I also worried about Oma and Opa, whose roles were diminished at camp. Now both in their sixties, they had endured many hardships earlier in their lives. As a young couple during WWI, they fled with their daughter to Estonia. There Opa was drafted by the Russian army. When the war ended, the family moved back to Riga, and Opa resumed his career at a bank. They bought their home in Mezparks during Latvia's prosperous years of independence. Expecting to return to their home at the end of WWII, the Soviet annexation of the Baltics had dashed those hopes.

True to Oma's nature, she easily made friends at camp.

Every day, she took her walks, visiting the other barracks to check in with neighbors. Still, there were few activities to keep her busy. There were no meals to prepare, few clothes to mend, or rabbits and gardens to tend.

Opa spent most of his days sitting on a bench in front of the barrack greeting passers-by. He had made good physical progress after his stroke, but with no access to a piano or cello, his musical skills declined. Since getting his silver flute, Opa, on occasion, carefully polished it. However, his dentures prevented him from being able to create a steady tone. Giving up, he would go outside, taking Maija with him. Watching our toddler sister became his primary pastime.

Our family started our second year at Camp Fischbach at the end of June 1946. Initially, UNRRA hadn't understood why so many refugee families refused to go back to their homelands. Homesick, some people did return, hoping to resume their lives. Many who went back were never heard from again.

Later we learned, the communist regime in control of the Baltics regarded those who left as traitors. Upon returning, they were given long prison sentences in Siberian work camps. There they often died of illness, starvation, and mistreatment thousands of miles from their homes.

In a short time, it became apparent to UNRRA that refugee repatriation wasn't a realistic goal. With longer refugee stays expected, UNRRA made efforts to improve the conditions in the camps. One of the first steps was to reorganize the system of DP camps throughout western Germany by nationality. At Camp Fischbach, around 500 refugees from Poland were moved to a Polish camp. From the 1,000 Latvians remaining, a committee was formed to work with UNRRA personnel to suggest improvements to the camp. In the following months,

Camp Fishbach became a whirlwind of activity as significant renovations took place.

Hurrying back from one of her neighborhood walks, Oma was filled with excitement.

"Did you hear? The barracks will now have permanent partitions to form four separate family units."

The blankets that once partitioned the barracks were re-purposed as curtains to be hung on the windows. Each living area received a wood-burning stove for heating and cooking. Rations traded in the village allowed families to plant flowers and vegetables around the buildings. Cages were created from discarded wire mesh to keep live chickens. The refurbished buildings couldn't replace the comforts of our former homes; however, now everyone referred to their barrack as their "cottage".

Oma and Opa stayed in one of the renovated barracks with the Bremanis next door. Father's and Mother's positions at the camp hospital became salaried, and our family was provided a brick duplex attached behind the hospital.

Other significant changes came. Our lunchtime routine of soup served from barrels between the barracks was replaced with a centralized kitchen for food and care packages. Classrooms were built in a brick storage facility and became our designated high school. The church and hospital also received renovations.

What was most appreciated, however, was the transformation of a vacant barn into an entertainment hall for concerts, plays, and dances. The programs were provided by professional actors and musicians, like the Bremanis, who lived in the camp. Even Latvians from surrounding camps came to attend. The changes couldn't have come a better time to create some normalcy in our lives and lift our spirits.

Our family's duplex was an improvement over the barracks, but it was still bare bones, having only two small bedrooms. A set of bunks took over most of Elga's and my room. Our parents' bedroom was slightly larger, allowing Mother to place a small mattress on the floor next to them for Maija's bed.

For me, the duplex's greatest asset was our access to the hospital's flush toilets and individual shower stalls. We needed to walk around to the front of the hospital to use the facilities, but it was a luxury compared to the pit toilets and shower barracks at the center of camp.

Our family became acquainted with our duplex neighbors, Dr. Anna Skendars and her family. She was the camp dentist and lived on the other side of us with her husband and daughter-in-law. Their son, drafted into the German army, had not survived one of the battles fought in Latvia.

Mother and our neighbor, Dr. Anna, became good friends. Underneath the duplex was a sizeable open cellar. A heap of tangled cords, wires, and telephone equipment gathered dust in one corner, evidence of a former switchboard. For several weeks, Mother and Dr. Anna saved both families' valuable cigarette rations with a plan in mind for the open space.

One day Elga and I walked in on Mother and Dr. Anna sitting at a table, counting out their saved coupons. I crossed my arms over my chest, looking at them.

"Just what are you planning to do with all of those rations?"

Narrowing her eyes, Elga added, "You two must be up to something."

With a gleam in her eye, Mother tilted her head and smiled, "You'll just have to wait and see."

The next day, we saw Mother and Dr. Anna coming up the road from the village. They were laughing and giggling like school girls as they took turns carrying something squealing and wiggling inside an old potato sack. Elga and I watched bewildered as they came toward the duplex.

"What in the world is going on?" Elga quizzed them as they approached.

"And what's in the bag?" I asked.

"Look for yourselves," Dr. Anna said, as she opened the top of the sack for us to see.

I peered inside and jumped back with a shriek, "Oh, my gosh! It's a piglet! What on earth are you doing with a piglet?"

Looking at us as if the answer was obvious, Mother replied, "What do you think people raise pigs and chickens for?"

Dr. Anna closed the bag and leaned in to make their intentions clear. With a smirk, she added, "We're going to fatten him up in the cellar, and then..."

She made a slashing motion across her neck. The two of them had decided the six-week-old piglet's fate. They'd raise it in the cellar, feeding it food scraps and leftover stale bread to fatten it up before completing the despicable deed.

Elga and I just shook our heads, silently agreeing not to take part in the scheme.

＊

About a dozen students prepared with us for the religious rite of confirmation in the Latvian church at camp. Mother and Dr. Anna planned to make it a special occasion for Elga and me.

"Girls, I have something special for your upcoming confirmation." Mother said, smiling with Dr. Anna as she beckoned to us.

She handed us each a package wrapped in brown paper.

Giving her perplexed looks, we tore the packages open, carefully lifting out beautiful long white silk dresses.

Holding the dress up, I was at a loss for words.

Finally, I sputtered, "They're beautiful!"

"I'm going to try mine on," Elga said, heading toward our room.

Following her in, I slipped the silk gown over my head, smoothing the soft, satiny fabric against my skin. Elga and I twirled around to look at each other as Mother and Dr. Anna peered in.

"You both look gorgeous!" Dr. Ana said as she and Mother entered.

Words caught in my throat as I looked at Mother and managed to utter, "We didn't expect anything like this!"

"Where did you get the dresses?" Elga gushed.

During the war, Allied soldiers often parachuted into the German countryside. Once the troops landed, they cut the chutes loose and left them in the fields to go into battle. Later, women from the villages retrieved the precious parachute silk. The material was a luxury and reaped a good profit. It was used to make gowns for weddings and special occasions like ours.

Mother discreetly saved our rations to trade for a used parachute. She then hired a seamstress to make the two confirmation gowns from the flowing, silk material. I'm sure Mother paid dearly with our family's saved coffee and cigarette rations to have our dresses made.

We were confirmed in our white silk dresses the following Sunday. After the ceremony, Dr. Anna's family, Oma and Opa, and the Bremanis came to our home for a celebratory dinner. Nearly everyone commented on how lovely Elga and I looked in our elegant dresses. However, the most enthusiastic praise was lavished on the delicious feast of roast pork that was served that afternoon.

DP camp barrack. Picture from Fisbachas Virsos by Ansis Pommers

Biruta and Elga in silk parachute dresses, Confirmation 1947

CHAPTER 13
Camp Fischbach & High School

At Camp Fischbach high school, Elga and I developed many close friendships. As the only twins, we were a novelty and simply known as "the sisters".

Some students came to the high school by train from as far away as Munich about 100 miles south. The students stayed in camp housing during the school week and commuted home for the weekends. One of those commuting students was Veltina, who became one of my best friends. Coincidentally, Veltina was from Riga. Her cousin, Aija, had been one of Elga's and my classmates in Mezparks. Veltina's family had lived near the city center, and our paths had never crossed in Riga. Her family fled Latvia around the same time we had.

Veltina was pretty, with blond hair, blue eyes, and a dimple in her chin. She was one of the smartest students in our class. When we first met, I delighted in discovering our mutual ties to her cousin Aija. Sadly, I learned Aija and her family never made it out of Riga before the Soviets returned, and their fate remained unknown.

Elga and I also became good friends with Annele, a student who lived at Camp Valka. It was a smaller camp about a 20-minute walk on the other side of the forest. Annele lived with her parents and two older brothers there. The family had come from a rural area of Latvia.

Annele walked back and forth to Camp Fischbach for school every day. She had soft brown waves of shoulder-length hair that framed her eyes and face. The three of us, Annele, Elga, and I, spent almost every weekend together. Elga was drawn to Annele's outgoing nature, and they became close.

At the end of each grueling school week, the three of us made every effort to get out of camp. Our parents would give us our family's cigarette rations to trade for train tickets. Nuremberg was only one stop and a few minutes away, and we rode the train there on the weekends.

Nuremberg had been heavily bombed toward the end of the war, but the city had made efforts to revitalize its central district. We loved going to the movies. Elga and I weren't strangers to motion pictures. As children, we went with our parents to see the popular Shirley Temple pictures in Riga.

One of our heartthrobs, Stewart Granger, was starring in "Madonna of the Seven Moons". The three of us, Annele, Elga, and I, couldn't wait to see it. On the weekend we went, we walked into the theater late, and a newsreel had already begun. A short clip about American football, which we had never seen before, was showing.

When images of grown men tackling and falling on top of each other appeared, the three of us began giggling and whispering to each other in Latvian. We were soundly shushed and heard comments about "those damned foreigners," and other insults erupt from the darkness. My temperature rose, and I felt the pain and indignity of being an outsider. Immediately, we stopped speaking Latvian and sat up in our seats, quieting until the movie began. At the first glimpse of Stewart Granger's face flashing before us, my embarrassment and anger melted away, but the awful memory lingered.

❧

Annele had two older brothers, John and Klavs, both in their twenties. Klavs, the younger of the two, was close to Annele. Klavs worked in Nuremberg for the Allies, providing security for jailed Nazi war prisoners. His required uniform was a military-style, long-sleeved black shirt and tie, which made him look menacing. We teased him incessantly, calling him "the black guard". Even so, he enjoyed spending his days off with us and often accompanied us on outings.

A favorite haunt for our group of friends was Dutzendteich, the vast stadium Hitler had built to hold his political rallies. It was a half-hour walk for us beyond the woods. It was now a sports complex holding motorcycle and car races, but the races didn't hold our interest.

Dutzendteich also held regular track competitions between the Latvian DP camps in the area. There we met other young people our age. For a short time, Elga even developed a relationship with a track star from another camp. Dutzendteich also had an Olympic size swimming pool. On warm summer days, we went there to swim and hang out with our friends.

Sam was another member in our group of friends. A classmate of ours from school at Camp Fischbach, he was from the city of Liepaja, Latvia. It was a port city south of Riga on the Baltic Sea near the Lithuanian border. He had also escaped with his family to Germany.

Sam was tall and lean with light brown hair and warm, welcoming eyes. His mischievous grin belied his philosophical nature. When I wasn't spending my weekend with Elga and Annele, Sam and I would take long walks in the forest bordering the camp or picnic in the tall grasses to talk about life and dream about our futures.

As good friends, Sam and I sometimes took off on excursions of our own. He wanted to investigate more of Nuremberg, a city rich in culture and history. In school, we had learned that Hitler considered Nuremberg the ideological center of Nazi Germany. It was said to be Hitler's favorite city.

In a bombing raid toward the end of the war, the Allies destroyed much of Nuremberg. One of its most famous buildings, the Imperial Castle and its church, sat on a ridge in the center of the town. It had been built in 1027 by the Holy Roman Empire and rebuilt in the 13th century. It suffered great damage during the Allied bombings. Sam convinced me to go with him to explore the site.

When we arrived at the castle, mountains of debris stood around it as if it had been recently bombed. We climbed a pile of rubble and, upon reaching the top, looked down on a massive area of ruin. Only the supporting structures of a few buildings remained.

The sight of so much historical and cultural destruction

took my breath away. I could only imagine the castle's former grandeur. Numbed by the scene, Sam and I stood immobilized for several minutes and said nothing. Solemnly, we climbed back down the pile of debris. Walking to the train station, we boarded the train and rode to camp in silence.

At high school, we had studied the German "Blitz" in London in 1940 and the obliteration of Stalingrad in 1942 and 1943. Now four years after the war, we came face-to-face with the aftermath of Nuremberg's 1945 bombing. We had just seen one small facet of the devastation inflicted by war. It didn't even take into account the human toll. The losses all seemed so pointless.

❧

Although Elga and I had considerable freedom, we still needed to provide our parents with details of our plans before going outside the camp. A big dance was coming up at neighboring Camp Valka. Elga, typically the more persuasive, went to ask our parents if we could go. A few minutes later, she returned, grinning with her thumbs up.

On the day of the dance, we rushed to get ready and planned to meet Ligita, another classmate, and Sam at the Gasthaus, a local pub midway between Camp Fischbach and Camp Valka. We gathered there occasionally for birthdays and special events, but tonight we were in a hurry to get to the dance.

When we arrived, the dance was in full swing. Two accordionists were belting out a lively folk tune. We saw Annele standing by the punch bowl, where the young people tended to congregate, and went to join her. She greeted us as we approached.

"I was getting worried. I thought you might not be able to come."

"Oh, you know how parents are," Elga said over the din of the music. "Sometimes, it takes a little convincing."

The stomping of feet on the dance floor, caused Annele to shout, "Klavs came tonight with some of his 'black guard' friends. They're standing across the room from us." Nodding her head in their direction, she added, "and several of them are very good looking."

She hadn't finished her sentence before Klavs came up to her with one of his co-workers.

"Annele, I'd like you to meet my friend, Arturs, and I don't know why," Klavs teased, "but he's been wanting to meet you."

Arturs made a slight bow and reached his hand out to Annele.

"Do you care to dance?" he asked.

Annele blushed, taking his extended hand as the two of them proceeded to the dance floor. They joined the others already doing a lively polka.

A classmate came over to ask me to dance. Soon we were laughing and dancing with the rest of them. As I whirled around, I caught a glimpse of Sam still standing by the punch bowl, tapping his foot to the beat of the music. He didn't dance, but as he stood there with his disarming grin, I thought to myself, "He'd make some young lady a handsome catch" and almost regretted that we were just friends. After the third polka with my dance partner, I was out of breath.

"Thank you for the dance, but I need to get some punch," I said, walking toward my friends by the refreshments.

Annele was grinning from ear-to-ear and chattering to Elga about Arturs. He had stepped away with his friends for a moment but came back to stand next to Annele, putting his arm around her waist as she leaned into him. When the music started, Annele and Arturs went back out on the dance floor, and we paid no further attention to them.

After a while, Klavs came over to us, frowning, "You haven't seen Annele and Arturs, have you? I think I've lost my best friend. I don't care so much about my little sister," Klavs joked, but we heard the concern in his voice.

We hadn't seen them, shrugged our shoulders, and shook our heads "no". As Klavs walked away, Ligita discreetly motioned to Elga and me to go outside. The three of us stood in the chilly night air with the dance music playing in the background. Ligita addressed us in hushed tones.

"I just saw Annele and Arturs coming out from the laundry barrack together," Ligita giggled. "You don't think either one of them was doing their laundry tonight, do you?"

"They're being awfully bold, don't you think?" I whispered.

"Yeah, I wonder what they were doing in there alone," Elga said sarcastically.

We returned inside. A few minutes later, Annele and Arturs came back into the dance hall, holding hands and gazing into each other's eyes. We were alarmed to see them so open with their affection. To think they might have stolen away for a kiss or something more was shocking. We said nothing to the others.

After that evening, Arturs spent more time with our group, but Annele and Arturs always managed to find a way to wander off on their own. When we went for a hike in the woods, they would go hand-in-hand in the opposite direction for a picnic in the fields. When we went to a dance, they would steal away before anyone knew they had left.

Several weeks later, Elga pulled me aside into our

bedroom. She grabbed me by the shoulders and placed her face close to mine.

"Annele just told me something she hasn't told anyone but me. You promise you can't say a word."

"I promise," I said, furrowing my brows, wondering if Elga was being overly dramatic.

"She's pregnant."

At first, I thought I hadn't heard correctly, but then the words registered. Annele and Arturs had been intimate with each other! I felt my stomach turn, but then I thought about Annele.

"Oh, no, what is she going to do?"

"They're talking about getting married."

"What? When? We only have a couple of weeks left of school before we graduate," I said.

"They're talking soon, even before we graduate," Elga said.

I staggered back with the news. One of our best friends was having a baby! Elga and I weren't ignorant about where babies came from. Oma raised rabbits in Mezparks, and, as children, we had seen what rabbits do. Oma explained how babies were created, and now "it" had happened to Annele.

At first, Annele's parents weren't happy about her pregnancy and her plans to marry so soon. She would have to leave school before her graduation. However, it had become more and more common that students left early when immigration opportunities arose. Annele would be allowed to take her exams early and get her diploma.

Through Klavs' friendship and work with Arturs, Annele's parents knew Arturs well and liked him. They came to accept the idea of Annele's marriage. Over the next few weeks, they were busy helping the couple make plans for their wedding.

Annele and Arturs were married on an early spring day filled with sunshine and a crisp chill in the air. The snows had recently melted, leaving its wet traces on the ground. The small wedding with close friends and family was held in Annele's parents' home at Camp Valka.

Elga and I wore our silk dresses, and our group of friends gathered for the wedding processional. Elga was the maid of honor, and Klavs was the best man. As a bridesmaid, I was paired with Max, one of Klavs and Artur's other good friends from the guards.

It was an occasion filled with mixed emotions. I was happy for Annele and Arturs, but there were also feelings of sadness and loss. A few days earlier, Annele had announced she and Arturs would be leaving for Australia. Arturs had been accepted for a job there, and their immigration papers approved. Annele's entire family started their own immigration paperwork, hoping they all could start new lives together in Australia.

After the wedding, Max and I began seeing each other regularly and spent a lot of time together. On a lazy Sunday afternoon, I was alone in the front room, sitting at the table, procrastinating over my math studies. I daydreamed and gazed out the window at the buds emerging from the trees. Elga had taken Maija, now almost five, for a short walk to visit some friends. Father and Mother were reading in their room.

I heard Mother's footsteps approach.

"Oh good, Biruta, you're not busy yet," she said. "I wanted to talk to you."

"Sure," I said, sitting up straighter, wondering why we needed to talk. "I was just taking a break before starting my schoolwork."

"That's what I wanted to talk to you about, school. You'll be graduating soon, and Father and I haven't heard any plans from you. Elga has talked to us about starting medical school."

"Well, I have thought about it," I said, "but I'm not sure. I like math and drafting. I'm thinking about architecture."

"Architecture?" Mother said. "Where would you go to school for that?"

"I don't know," I said, starting to bristle. "I know Elga is thinking about the University in Munich. I'm sure they have classes in architecture."

"Biruta, Father and I are only receiving a small stipend for our work. We may get additional educational benefits for you and Elga, but not much. I'm afraid we can't afford to send both of you to the university. Besides, how practical would a job in architecture be? You need to be employable in order for our family to emigrate."

"But what about Annele? She went to Australia without a job," I argued.

"Annele is now Arturs' wife," Mother emphasized, "and he does have a job."

Mother hesitated and then frowned as if a thought had just occurred to her.

"You're not making any plans with Max, are you?"

"No, Mother, we're just friends," I stated flatly as my face reddened. My throat began to tighten, and I lowered my eyes, refusing to look at her.

"Well, Father and I have been concerned where things are going with you two. We're still planning to emigrate as a family. It might be a good idea to cool that relationship."

I was seething by now.

Mother stopped for a moment and then continued, "He's also several years older than you and may have other ideas."

"Mother!" I said, my voice rising. "He's only four years older! Besides, I'm not Annele, and I'm not your precious Elga either!"

I was shouting by now. I got up and ran to my room. I brushed by Oma, who was just coming in.

As I slammed my door shut, I heard Oma ask Mother, "What was that all about?"

I didn't wait to hear Mother's reply. I threw myself on my bed and cried long, heaving sobs coming from the depths within me. For the last four years, I'd been living in this horrid camp and been pushed to my limits. Mother didn't really know or understand me. Who was she to crush my dreams?

I was wallowing in my self-pity when I heard the bedroom door creak open. Hardly able to focus through my tears, I saw it was Oma. She slipped in next to me, sat on my bed, and rubbed my back.

Oma began humming a tune and then sang it in German. The song was familiar to me.

Auf die Berge mocht ich fliegen,
Mochte sehn ein grunes Tahl.
Mocht in Gras and Blumen liegen
Und mich freun am Sonnenstrahl [10]

(Loosely translated)
I want to fly to the mountains,
And see the green valley
May I lie in grass and flowers
And delight in the sunshine.

Her sweet voice soothed me and quieted my anger. My sobs tapered off as I sat up into her embrace. She sang the song again. Her gentle voice and caress were familiar. She rocked me like she did when I was a little girl. Oma understood me and my longing for something better than this basic existence. I wanted to get on with my life. I wanted to get out of this camp.

CHAPTER 14

Fischbach Part II,

The International Refugee Organization (IRO)

The IRO gained full responsibilities of the camps in July 1947. It is estimated that 600,000 displaced persons and 900,000 refugees lived in the camps when the IRO took operational responsibilities.[11]

I nitially, the Germans welcomed foreign refugees into their country as substitute workers for those missing, disabled, or killed during the war. Those who found employment often resettled into the community to live. However, Germany couldn't absorb all the refugees, and only a few countries were accepting immigrants.

UNRRA's goal was to assist refugees back to their home countries. When it became clear that it could no longer be an objective, the International Relief Organization (IRO) took over. Its goal was to assist refugees toward emigration and resettlement rather than repatriation. It meant longer stays in the DP camps while resettlements to other countries were coordinated.

To aid in resettlement, the IRO provided training and salaried employment. My parents started getting a regular salary for their work at the hospital. Our family moved from the duplex to a larger, renovated barrack, allowing Oma and Opa to move back in with us.

Father worked tirelessly with the IRO looking at resettlement options for our family. Through letters, he also reconnected with a cousin who had emigrated to South America after WWI. She lived in a Latvian community and worked on a coffee and sugar plantation in Sao Paulo, Brazil. Opportunities to work were there, and Father applied to the Brazilian consulate for visas for our family.

Several weeks later, Father received a letter from the Brazilian consulate. Our initial visa application was approved. We were overjoyed. There was a glimmer of hope that our family might find a permanent home and be able to leave Camp Fischbach.

"It's good news, but it's only the first step," Father cautioned. "We'll have to wait to be called to a resettlement camp for additional screening before official visas are granted."

"When might that be?" Mother asked.

"I'm not sure," Father said. "Tens of thousands of refugees are hoping to immigrate, so we will have to wait until we are notified. I'm told the screening process itself will take a few days."

Several weeks passed until, finally, our family was told to report to a resettlement camp nearby. We packed to leave for the camp the next day.

On the first day, Mother, Father, Oma, and Opa were called for interviews while Elga and I waited in our room with Maija.

When they returned, Elga and I bombarded our parents with questions, "Tell us! What did they all want to know?"

"They asked why we left Latvia, about our political views, and where we've been staying in Germany. The expected things," Father said.

Mother added, "They basically reviewed our whole life history: where we went to school, where we lived and worked in Latvia, and if we'd ever been imprisoned for any reason."

"Well, have you?" Elga teased.

I scowled at Elga, nudging her in her side, then turned to address Father and Mother, "So, what happens next?"

"Tomorrow, we'll all get physical exams and x-rays to rule out any illness or disease," Father explained, "and then we return to Fischbach to wait."

In a few days, the interviews and exams were completed, and we returned to Camp Fischbach. We waited several more weeks before hearing anything. Then arriving home from school one day, Elga and I were greeted at the front door by Oma and Opa. Oma waved an official-looking letter in her hand addressed to Father.

Talking in a rush of words, she exclaimed, "We went to the IRO offices today to get the mail, and this arrived! It's from the Brazilian consulate!"

Elga and I contemplated running to the hospital to give Father the letter. However, in a few minutes, he and Mother would be returning from work. So instead, we decided to wait, all of us trying to contain our excitement.

As soon as my parents walked in the door, Elga and I ran to Father. We shoved the letter at him, crowding around him to find out what it said. With Mother looking over his shoulder, Father tore the letter open. They scanned it together in silence. Staring at their faces, we looked for any clues as to what the letter said.

"What does it say, Hermanis?" Oma pleaded.

At first, Father's face beamed, but as he looked at the next page, his face fell.

"Our visas have been approved," he said, turning to Mother with a worried look.

"That's wonderful news!" Oma exclaimed, "but why the concern?"

"Our immediate family's application has been approved," Father said and stopped. He lowered his head and the letter.

Turning to look Oma and Opa, he said, "but yours have been denied."

A long silence hung in the room.

Then Mother cried out, "How can that be? We all applied together as one family!"

Looking at Mother, Father tried to explain. "The letter says they're being denied because of their ages. It is unlikely they would be able to work to provide for themselves. Elsa, we're the only two wage earners supporting our family of seven."

Mother sank into a chair and moaned, "What will we do? From the beginning, we've planned for the entire family to stay together."

Putting a hand on Mother's shoulder, Father said, "All may not be lost. Right now, the girls are still in high school. When they graduate in a few months and get additional work training, they'll be considered wage earners, too. We can reapply for Oma and Opa's visas then. We'll just have to wait."

Although it appeared to be a solution, it was still a blow to our family. With the letter, our immediate hopes to leave Camp Fischbach and find a permanent home had vanished.

Several weeks later, Opa became ill with pneumonia. Oma went to his bedside to care for him day and night. When I passed their room, I could hear their soft voices and Opa's weak laughter as they reminisced. I saw Father and Mother in the hall, talking together in hushed tones and heard Mother's voice break as she tried to remain stoic. She was asking Father if there was anything more medically that could be done for Opa.

The next day, we were taken aback at how quickly Opa had taken a turn for the worse. He seldom stirred as his fever spiked, and he struggled to breathe, his chest rattling with every breath. Several times, we attempted to relieve a weary-looking Oma, but she refused, her frail fingers intertwining with Opa's on top of the bedcovers. As she had done once before, Oma began singing hymns to Opa in her soft, lilting voice and praying over him. We left the room to allow them to be alone together.

Later that evening, Elga and I were preparing for bed when we heard a grief-stricken wail echoing through the hall. We ran to Oma and Opa's bedroom to find Father and Mother already standing there. Father checked Opa's heart rate and pulse, then sadly shook his head. We stood by forlorn as Oma fell onto Opa's chest and wept with abandon. After several minutes we gently pulled Oma away, encircling her in our arms. We consoled not only her but ourselves as we mourned Opa's passing.

Opa died on March 3, 1949, at the age of 71. The funeral service was held at the small church in the center of the camp with the Lutheran minister presiding. Opa was well known for his love of music, and all the local camp musicians, including Janis and Aina Bremanis, came to play at his service. Upon hearing Opa's favorite songs, Elga and I held onto each other and cried openly.

Opa was laid to rest in a small cemetery just outside the gates of the camp. A small marker identified his grave. He was buried with all the other refugees who had died at Camp Fischbach over the past four years. All of their collective hopes to see their Latvian homeland again would never come to pass.

In the days following Opa's funeral, fond memories of him came flooding back to me. It wasn't fair. Despite his stroke, Opa had been so agreeable in coming with us to Germany. Now, he could never go home to Latvia or go forward with our family as we resettled. I brushed away a tear from the corner of my eye as Elga entered our room.

"I just can't get over that Opa isn't with us anymore," I said to her.

"I know," Elga replied with a pained expression. "He was so much a part of our lives. Remember our music lessons with Opa? When we left Riga, we couldn't bring his violin. It was silly, but I kept one of the strings to remind me of Opa's music."

"When I think of Opa, I think of how he loved the trees surrounding their Mezparks home and at Alexander Heights," I said. "After everything we've been through, it's just not right that he's not with us anymore or that he'll never see Riga again. I wish there were something more we could do."

"What do you mean?" Elga asked.

"Well, like a special tribute or memorial to him from us."

We sat for a moment thinking and then I had an idea.

"Elga, get your violin string. If Opa can't be with us, we can at least leave some of our memories with him."

Elga found the string, and I rummaged through my satchel of childhood keepsakes. At the bottom, I found what I was looking for.

"Look, Elga. It's a chestnut from outside our bedroom window at Alexander Heights. We can leave something of us and Riga with Opa."

"Sometimes you're a little crazy, Biruta, but I think it would be a fitting remembrance."

Elga and I took our keepsakes and walked to Opa's marker at the cemetery. Next to it, we dug a small, shallow hole. Inside it, Elga coiled her violin string from Mezparks, and I placed the chestnut from Alexander Heights. We covered them and stood in silence for a few moments over Opa's grave.

"We're going to miss you, Opa," Elga said.

"I wish you'd still be coming with us. At least now, you'll always have a part of us with you."

Putting our arms around each other, Elga and I strolled back to camp.

Decades later, I was able to return to Camp Fischbach. The entire camp had been dismantled, and the site sat empty. Nothing remained to indicate that at one time, over 1,500 refugees had lived here. Even the individual grave markers in the cemetery were gone. Only a single monument stood to commemorate all the Displaced Persons who died at Camp Fischbach and were unable to go home.

CHAPTER 15
Munich

E lga and I graduated from Camp Fishbach high school in
the spring of 1949. To ensure the German universities
would recognize our diplomas, we took exams with their
Department of Education and passed. Father and Mother
persuaded both of us to get certified as nurses' aides. Obtaining
the certification would make us more employable and aid in
our family's relocation. The program consisted of two and
a half months of classroom studies and another three and a
half months of practical experience. We would finish before
Christmas, and our parents would re-apply for visas to Brazil.

Elga and I, along with one of our classmates, Ligita, applied
for nurses' aide classes at an IRO hospital in Munich. We were
all accepted into the program. My dreams of becoming an
architect were put on hold.

A decision also had to be made regarding my relationship
with Max. Juggling his work hours in Nuremberg, my classes in

Munich, and the train schedules between the two cities would leave us little time to be together. We agreed to part ways.

In June, Elga, Ligita, and I said good-bye to our families in Camp Fischbach and boarded a train for Munich. We looked forward to this new phase in our lives and being on our own in a big city. At the Munich station, the new students were met and taken to the teaching hospital.

Once at the hospital, we were led to the nursing dorm on the third floor. There we were given strict rules: a curfew with lights out and absolutely no smoking, drinking, or men allowed on the floor. An infraction could mean expulsion from the program. Nuns supervised us, enforced the rules, and taught our classes.

On the floor, there were a total of 20 nursing students assigned to two large rooms. Each room held 10 students, with a single bed and desk for each of us. At the far end of the hallway, a lounge with couches, a small library, and radio was available for our free time. We had very little of it, once classes began.

After a few weeks of rigorous classes, I missed my family at Fishbach. From time to time, however, Father and Mother took the train to Munich to attend seminars at the hospital. The courses, organized by the IRO, updated refugee physicians on medical practices and advances. It would improve their prospects of resettlement in other parts of the world. A particular two-week course interested Mother, and she saw it as an opportunity to check in on us.

Mother was at the first day of her seminar while I was assisting on the hospital floors. A small group of doctors approached and gathered around a patient's bed with whom I'd been working. I stepped aside while they examined the chart and the patient. I noticed one of the young physicians staring at me. He was tall and dark-haired with piercing blue eyes. I flashed a smile and looked down, waiting for the group to move on. As they left, the young doctor lingered in the doorway, looking as if he wished to speak to me.

"Pardon me, doctor, do you have a question?" I asked. "If not, I need to attend to others."

"I'm sorry, no," he stammered. "I'll let you get back to your duties."

He then went to join his group.

Mildly irritated, I took my files and left the room for my next patient. I was anxious to finish my work and looked forward to seeing Mother. In no time, I had forgotten the incident. At the end of my shift, I rushed for my locker and was thrown off guard when I saw the same young doctor in the hallway outside the nurses' area.

"Excuse me," he said, addressing me. "I was hoping to find you here. I wanted to apologize. I didn't mean to disturb you while you were working."

He glanced at my name tag.

"Biruta," he said out loud, his face brightening and eyes sparkling. "That's a Latvian name. I thought I heard you speaking Latvian to one of the patients. You're Latvian, yes?"

Taken by surprise, I simply nodded.

Switching from German to Latvian, he then said, "Pardon me, I've forgotten my manners. I'm Karlis Zvejnieks, from Ventspils. When I heard Latvian spoken on the hospital floor, I was startled. Then I was doubly surprised when I looked up to see the words coming from such a lovely young nurse."

I blushed. Even if he was from Latvia, I didn't want to get into a long-winded conversation. Many of the doctors, including the married ones, often flirted with the young nurse trainees, expecting to gain their favor. Mother and Elga were waiting for me.

"Thank you. Yes, my family and I are from Riga," I replied. "But I'm sorry, I'm in a hurry. My mother is visiting, and she and my sister are expecting me. Perhaps another time?"

"Another time then. I hope to see you again soon."

"Yes," I said as I dashed off to meet Mother and Elga.

The next day, I didn't see the young doctor at the hospital and thought nothing of it. I was already looking forward to the weekend with Mother, Elga, and Ligita. We were going on an excursion with some of the seminar doctors to Berchtesgaden, Hitler's Eagle's Nest. It was in the Alps on the German and Austrian border only two hours south of Munich. It was said to be a spectacularly beautiful area.

"That's great! We haven't had a break from classes since we've been here," I said when Mother told us about the excursion.

Some Latvian doctors from the seminar rented a large van for about a dozen medical staff. We would stay at a Latvian DP camp near Berchtesgaden overnight. The morning of the trip, Elga, Ligita, and I got in the van with Mother. Sitting in my seat, I looked up and was shocked to see Dr. Zvejnieks running toward the vehicle. Boarding, he didn't see us and sat down. Once seated, he looked up and saw me. He nodded, and I smiled. I then continued chatting with Elga, Ligita, and Mother about the news from Fishbach and our experiences at the hospital.

We reached our first stop and got out to stretch our legs. Dr. Zvejnieks approached us.

"Excuse me, Dr. Riesbergs," he said, addressing Mother, and then looked at me. "I met this young nurse's aide on the hospital floor the other day. Is she with you?"

"Yes, Dr. Zvejnieks, this is my daughter, Biruta, her twin sister Elga, and their friend Ligita. All three of them are in nurses' aide training at the hospital," she said with a smile. "For me, the seminar was an opportunity to visit and catch up with them."

"What a pleasant surprise. I could never have guessed these two young ladies were your daughters," he replied, returning her smile.

Addressing me, he said, "Biruta, I'm so delighted to see you again."

Then speaking to all of us, "Since we're all on holiday together, please, call me Karlis."

Then he left to join some of the other doctors.

When he was gone, Mother turned to me and asked, "You've met Dr. Zvejnieks before, Biruta?"

"Yes. Just the other day, on the hospital floor," I said.

"He's awfully handsome, and you never even told us about him," Elga teased.

"Why the big secret?" Ligita chimed in.

"No secret," I said. "He was just making rounds with the other doctors, and it didn't seem very newsworthy."

The four of us walked back to the van to continue our journey to Eagle's Nest. Climbing the winding roads, we gazed out the windows, overcome with the beauty of the Alps. When we reached our destination, we got out to hike and take in the grandeur of the mountains, lakes, and forests around Berchtesgaden. In the evening, we took our meals at the Latvian DP camp. Soon after, weary from hiking in the fresh mountain air, we fell into our beds.

The next morning at breakfast, Karlis made a point to come over to us to say, "Good morning." Since I had just taken a bite to eat and had my mouth full, I only nodded and smiled.

After he left, Mother asked, "Why didn't you say anything to Dr. Zvejnieks? He seems like such a nice young man."

"He told us to call him Karlis," Elga reminded her.

"I had food in my mouth," I objected. "I couldn't say anything."

"I noticed he couldn't take his eyes off you yesterday," Ligita smirked.

"We've been so busy sightseeing, and he's been with the other doctors. I really hadn't noticed."

"Well, you could be nicer to him," Elga said with a sly grin.

"OK," I said, shrugging my shoulders, but thinking to myself that I hadn't come to Munich looking for a relationship.

That morning we hiked some more, and by midday, everyone was ready to go back to Munich. Taking our seats on the van, I passed Karlis, making a point to greet him warmly.

"Weren't the German Alps amazing?" I gushed.

I turned back to look at Mother, Elga, and Ligita to be sure that they had heard me. Exhausted, I sat down and fell asleep on the way back to the hospital.

On the return trip, some people from the excursion organized a dinner party later that evening at the hospital. Mother, Elga, Ligita, and I joined everyone for the dinner. Karlis and some other physicians were already seated at another table.

After a dinner of socializing and reminiscing about our trip, the party broke up early. Everyone was exhausted by the full weekend, and most had the seminar to attend the next morning. Elga, Ligita, and I said good night to Mother, who returned to her room in the physicians' quarters. The three of us headed for our dorm, but as we left, I heard the clinking of glass. I looked over my shoulder to see a few of the doctors grabbing some unopened bottles of wine off the tables. Thinking nothing of it, we returned to our room.

Most of the nursing students were gone for the two-week break from our training. The entire dorm was almost empty as we entered our room. We, too, would go to Fischbach with Mother when her seminar was over.

Suddenly, we heard a commotion in the stairwell.

Cracking our door open, we looked out into the dim hallway to see two shadowy figures. They were speaking Latvian, and one was carrying a bottle of wine. They were doctors from our dinner party. As they moved down the hall toward our room, they successively knocked on doors along the way. It seemed they had come to the nurses' dorm looking for some companions to continue their celebration.

Shaking our heads and chuckling, the three of us quietly pulled our door shut and stood behind it, listening. We didn't want to encourage them. A moment later, the footsteps stopped in front of our door.

"C'mon, we know you're in there," one of the doctors said and started knocking.

"Shhhh, no one's home," Ligita giggled from behind the safety of the door. "You need to leave before you get us into trouble."

Elga whispered to us, "The nuns must be gone. Otherwise, they'd be up here by now."

"Please, come out," the other doctor said, "We just want to talk to some girls from our homeland."

I recognized the voice. It was Karlis.

Fearful that someone would report us, we became quiet, hoping they would go away.

With no response from us, the first doctor grumbled, "Oh, what's the use. I guess I'll just take this bottle back to my room."

We heard one pair of footsteps retreating in the hall and going down the stairs – then silence.

I whispered to Elga and Ligita, "I think one of them was Karlis. Let me see if he's still out there."

"No, Biruta," Elga said firmly. "What if a nun comes back and sees you?"

"If they haven't heard anything by now, they're not here," I said, reaching for the door. "We'll go out on the fire escape so we won't be seen."

It was a ploy that had been used by some of the other nursing students.

"You're taking a big risk," Elga warned.

"I know. I'll be careful. Besides, you both insisted I should be nicer to Karlis."

I opened the door and went out. At first, I couldn't see as my eyes adjusted to the darkened hallway. Then I saw movement. A tall shadow stood up from sitting on the floor.

"Biruta, is that you?" Karlis said, trying to keep his voice low. "I've been wanting to talk to you alone and haven't had the chance."

I drew closer, and he continued, "You know, the first time I saw you wasn't at the hospital. It was earlier in the day. I was taking the streetcar, and there was a light drizzle. I caught a glimpse of a girl in a bright green raincoat and matching umbrella walking on the sidewalk. The coat and umbrella stood out in the gray mist. Then she turned around, and I saw the most beautiful girl I had ever seen. It was only a moment, but I knew I'd never forget her face."

He stopped for a moment to reach for my hand, "Imagine my surprise when a few hours later, I saw the very same girl in a nurse's uniform at the hospital. When she spoke Latvian, my heart almost stopped. It was you, Biruta."

In the semi-darkness, I was glad Karlis didn't see how deeply I was blushing. I nodded toward the window at the far end of the hall.

"Follow me to the fire escape. We can sit out there to talk."

Karlis smiled a sheepish grin, and followed me, "Are you sure it's alright?"

I shrugged my shoulders. "I don't think the nuns are here. They certainly would've heard the two of you knocking on doors. What were you thinking?"

"I only wanted to talk to you," Karlis said.

We reached the window, and he took my hand to steady me over the sill. Stepping out onto the fire escape, we sat without talking for a few moments. Huddled together against the cool night air, we looked at the night sky.

"Look, there's Orion, the Hunter, and Ursa, the bear," I said, pointing them out.

"Yes, it's amazing how the world can feel so right on a clear night like this," Karlis said, looking at me.

All of a sudden his tone changed.

"We're both a long way from home. How is it that you are here? I really want to know your story."

I told him how my family had gotten out of Latvia and fled to Germany, and that we had been at Camp Fischbach for the past four years. Talking about it amazed me how long it had been since we left Riga. I gazed at the stars again and wondered what they held for my future.

I sighed and looked at Karlis, "So, what's your story?"

"My family is from Ventspils. I'm 28, the oldest of six. I have two brothers, a sister, a half-brother, and half-sister. My father remarried after my mother died. I began school at the University in Riga to study philosophy and writing. After two years, I changed to medicine when the Russians took over. With war imminent, it seemed a more practical profession. During "the terrible year," we were required to take classes in communist doctrine in medical school. Can you imagine?"

"Yes, I remember having to write a poem in school praising Stalin and how upset Mother was."

Shaking his head, Karlis continued, "Later, when the Germans came into Latvia, they conscripted young Latvian men, like myself and my younger brother, Alfreds, into their army. As a medic, I was stationed in a field hospital on Latvia's eastern front."

"Oh, no! You must have seen awful things," I said, turning toward him.

"We were trying to save Latvian lives," he said, stopping to frown for a moment before going on. "When the Russians collapsed the Latvian front, the Germans retreated, taking us with them. At one time, I was stationed near the port of Danzig, Poland. Our job was to retrieve the bodies of refugees who had washed up on the shores of the Baltic Sea. Their ships had been sunk while fleeing the Soviets."

I shuddered. It had been the port our family had sailed to from Riga. I also thought back to our concerns for Father as he left for Germany.

I stared at Karlis and whispered, "I can't imagine the horrors you've seen."

He didn't say anything for a long while before going on.

"As Nazi war losses mounted, they retreated further into Germany. After the war and before things got sorted out, Latvians who were drafted into the German army were detained in Allied prisoner of war camps. I was held in Putlos prison in Belgium."

Our family's struggles could not compare to what Karlis had experienced. I remained silent.

"Anyway, to make a long story short," Karlis said, "I ended up in Greven DP camp near Munster. It's about a day's train ride northwest of here. As part of war reparations, German universities were required to accept a percentage of war refugees into their schools. Some friends and I completed medical school at Munster University. After three years, I only have a dissertation to write.

Like your mother, I'm taking a course in Munich to prepare for immigration. Then while riding on a streetcar one day, I saw a beautiful girl in a green raincoat who took my breath away," Karlis said as he lifted my chin to his face and looked into my eyes. "And here we are."

I shivered, and Karlis wrapped his jacket around me, mistaking me for being cold. I switched the subject, asking, "Do you have a plan for resettlement?"

"Actually, I do," he said thrusting his shoulders back. "I have an affidavit to work as a farmhand in Alexandria, Minnesota, in the United States of America. I'm waiting for my visa to get approved."

"A farmhand! You're a doctor!"

"Shhhh, don't tell anyone," Karlis said. "America needs farm help, and it's a way for me to get my foot in the door. I'm hoping to find other opportunities once I get there. What about your family?"

"It's complicated. It's why Elga and I are in nurse's aide training. Until we get work certificates, we're still considered our parents' dependents along with my grandmother and little sister. Father and Mother are the only two workers providing for our family of six. Father has a cousin in Brazil, and we're waiting to re-apply for visas once Elga and I finish our training."

"Brazil! That's not even close to Minnesota. I might have to do something about that," Karlis said, pulling me closer.

Thinking about our separate circumstances and not wanting to get too involved, I sighed and changed the subject.

"It's so peaceful out here, I'd like to stay out here all night, but it's getting late, and you have a seminar in the morning."

I got to my feet.

"Yes, I'm afraid you're right. After this past weekend, we both should get some sleep," Karlis took my hand to guide me back through the window and into the hall. He walked me back to my room, and we stood outside the door.

"Can we get together again before my two weeks are up in Munich? I know of a great restaurant-pub just up the street. When are you done with work tomorrow?"

"We're on a break," I said.

"Great. Dinner tomorrow night it is then, alright?"

"Yes, that would be nice," I said as I handed Karlis back his jacket.

Smiling, I said good night as he reached for my hand and kissed it. He then crept back down the stairs.

When I entered the room, I was surprised to see Elga had a light on and was reading in bed.

"What happened?" she asked.

"Oh, nothing. We just talked," I replied.

"Anything else?"

"He asked me out to dinner tomorrow night."

"Oh, Biruta, that's wonderful! But I'm tired, so you'll have to tell me more in the morning," she said as she turned out her light, rolled over, and went to sleep.

I got ready for bed and crawled under the covers, lying there for a moment. Karlis' flattery had set my mind spinning. I was sure he was just seeking some female companionship during his time in Munich. He would be returning to Munster in less than two weeks and then going to America. There could be nothing more for us. A long-term relationship was not in our stars. I rolled over to fluff up my pillow, turned out my light, and drifted off to sleep.

꧁

The following night, Karlis and I went to the Regina Café, a cozy, dimly lit restaurant with strolling musicians playing the popular songs of the day. We heard "Du bist die Rose" that night and later, hearing it again, decided to make it 'our song'. Over the next few days, Karlis scheduled almost every minute of his free time with me.

We discovered the Englischer Garten, a beautiful city park located in the center of Munich. Shaded walking paths, brooks, and ponds embellished the park. The Isar river, fed from the nearby Alps, flowed through it, and we rowed a boat on its waters while snow-white swans glided past. It was a paradise after years of living in a DP camp.

On our last weekend together, Karlis and I planned for a picnic and a day on the beach at Starnberg See, a large lake not far from Munich. That morning, the sun was shining brightly with not a cloud in the sky, promising a beautiful day. We agreed not to talk about our parting and packed a basket of food, our swimming clothes and then took the train from Munich to the lake.

Once there, we hopped on a ferry, stopping at various points to walk the paths or take a swim in the lake's refreshing waters. When we became tired, we lay in the shade of an enormous oak tree that lined the shore to admire the pure beauty of nature around us. Other times, we basked in the sunshine to take in its warming rays.

Beyond a walking path, Karlis noticed an open green meadow leading into a forest. Grabbing the picnic basket, he ran across the expanse of long grasses, and I followed behind him, laughing. The grasses brushed against my legs as I sprinted across the field. When I finally caught up to him, at the edge of the forest, we both fell to the ground, gasping to catch our breath.

We got up to walk hand-in-hand into the woods, marveling at the ancient pines. As we got to a clearing, we saw a grouping of mushrooms with large brown caps growing on the forest floor under a stand of spruce trees.

"Oh, look!" Karlis exclaimed. "Baravika mushrooms, my favorite. My step-mother used to cook them all the time. I haven't eaten them in ages."

"The last time I saw them, I was a little girl in Mezparks," I said. "Apparently, no one has been here lately; otherwise, they would've been picked."

We marveled at our good fortune and gathered as many mushrooms as we could. Not having anything to carry them, we bundled the mushrooms into the cloth napkins I had brought for our picnic.

The sun was fading, and we hadn't yet been to the main promenade. We hid our "treasure" behind a tree and hurried to the shops. Karlis was buying me sweets and balloons when we heard the horn for the last ferry to the train station. We ran toward the dock when Karlis suddenly remembered the mushrooms. We raced to the tree and back to the boat. Faces flushed from our sprint and a day in the sun, we fell into our seats just as the ferry pulled away from the pier. I laid my head in Karl's shoulder as we rode back to the train station, exhausted but happy.

Karlis and I arrived back at the hospital, hungry to eat our mushrooms. However, we didn't have anywhere to cook them. Neither the dorm nor Karlis' room had any cooking facilities. I remembered the ward kitchens on each hospital floor. Elga had volunteered for an evening shift. Maybe she would let us in. Finding her, we explained what we wanted to do. She rolled her eyes and reluctantly agreed.

In the kitchen, we unwrapped and washed what Karlis called our "catch of the day". Discovering some butter in the icebox, I used it to saute the mushrooms. The earthy scent of them sizzling and frying in the butter made our mouths water. Their aroma permeated the kitchen and wafted onto the ward, causing Elga to poke her head around the door.

"Really, Biruta, you can smell the mushrooms throughout the whole hospital. I'm going to get in trouble," she said, stomping over to the window, throwing it open, and going back to her work.

Karlis and I stifled a laugh as we continued to fry the last of the mushrooms. He stood behind me, putting his arms around my waist.

"Frying mushrooms always reminded me of my mother's cooking, but now it will remind me of something else."

"Oh, really?" I grinned. "What?"

"It will remind of you and our wonderful day together," Karlis said as he nibbled my ear.

"You're tickling me, have these instead," I said, emptying the pan onto a plate.

We savored each bite together and saved a few for Elga. I never knew how the ward supervisor hadn't noticed our cooking.

❧

It was the end of August. The two-week physician's seminar in Munich was over. Mother was returning to Fischbach by train. Elga and I would join her for the rest of our break, and Karlis was going back to his DP camp outside of Munster.

Before Karlis left, he wanted to stop to see his younger brother, Alfreds, at the Augsburg DP camp just north of Munich. His brother told him there was a garden party and dance taking place on the day he planned to come. Karlis invited me to go. I could go to the party and join Mother and Elga on the train as it passed through Augsburg en-route to Fishbach. Mother permitted me to go.

Karlis and I left Munich on the early afternoon train to Augsburg. Alfreds met us at the station and greeted us with a hug. He was a slighter version of Karlis with a thin frame. I imagined it was the price he had paid for being a prisoner of war.

At the camp, Alfreds led us to a shaded outdoor area set with tables and chairs where drinks and snacks were served. Others were already mingling there. We found a table and soon after introductions were made, I felt at ease with the two brothers. I joined in as we reminisced about Latvia, family, and where the war had taken us. We spent the entire afternoon talking and laughing.

At dusk, the colored lanterns hanging in the trees were lit, and the orchestra assembled. Soon, the soft sound of violins and cellos began drifting through the air. In my chair, I gently swayed to the music. Karlis took my hand, leading me to the makeshift dance floor while Alfreds met up with other friends.

As the sky darkened, one-by-one, stars appeared and sparkled on the party-goers below. Karlis and I danced for several numbers. Carried away by the dream-like atmosphere, I rested my head on his shoulder. With a sweeping motion, Karlis turned and led me behind the orchestra stage. Alone and hidden from view, Karlis took both my hands into his and turned to face me, gazing into my eyes.

"Biruta, I can't lose you. Will you marry me?"

The words took a moment to register. After regaining my senses, my mind reeled. We had only known each other for less than two weeks. The last several days had been magical, but from the beginning, I hadn't expected our relationship to go beyond our time in Munich. Our paths were leading us in different directions. I planned to go with my family to Brazil while Karlis had a job waiting for him in America. He was 28 and soon a full-fledged physician. I was 19, unsure of my goals, and certainly not ready for marriage.

"Karlis, I don't know what to say," I stammered. "It's all so sudden. I didn't see this coming. I've loved our time together. I never thought of anything beyond our time in Munich. Our futures are so uncertain. I can't think right now and need some time."

Karlis grabbed me, clutched me in his arms, and held me close. He took my face in his hands and leaned down to kiss me. My heart stirred.

"Biruta, you know I love you. I will wait for you for as long as it takes. I believe in love at first sight, and I know in my heart, you are the one."

I was numb as Karlis led me by the hand back to the dance floor. We danced a few more dances, but my head was in a fog. The party ended. The evening had been a fairy tale, but Karlis' proposal had shaken me to the core. In a short while, I would be joining Mother and Elga on the train returning to Fischbach.

We walked arm-in-arm to the train station. I stood beside Karlis on the platform, avoiding his gaze as we waited for the train. It was hard saying good-bye, not knowing when we would see each other again and what answer I would give him.

As the northbound train from Munich rolled into the station, Karlis held me in a long embrace and whispered in my ear.

"Promise me you'll write. Remember, I'll be waiting for your answer."

I nodded my assurance.

In a puff of steam, the train stopped, and the conductor shouted "All aboard" as the doors opened. Our hands drifted apart as I turned to go. I stood on the top step looking back to smile at Karlis. Others were waiting to board, so I pivoted and, in a daze, entered the train, shouldering my bag between the row of seats.

Through one of the windows, I caught a glimpse of Karlis still standing on the platform. I weakly raised my hand to wave, but he could no longer see me. Sadness and confusion swept over me.

I shifted my gaze inside the train compartment and began searching for Mother and Elga. Elga waved her arms above her, catching my attention. I got to my seat as the train blew one long piercing whistle and started to pull away from the station. I looked to see Karlis one last time and saw he had turned to walk away, his tall silhouette fading as the train picked up speed.

I sat down by Mother and Elga, taking a seat by the window. Noticing that something was amiss, Elga asked, "How was your evening with Karlis?"

"It was wonderful," I said, closing my eyes.

"Wonderful? Then why look so sad?"

I hesitated before I replied. "He asked me to marry him, and I don't know what to do."

Mother overheard.

"Marry you?" she repeated with a surprised look on her face.

"Yes," I said, "I know. We've only known each other for less than two weeks."

"Do you care for him?" Mother asked.

"Yes, of course, I do," I said.

"Well then, why not?"

I was taken aback by her straightforward reply and couldn't answer. I looked out the window at the dark landscape flying by. Was it that simple? At the moment I was so unsure of myself. Elga reached over to squeeze my hand. The gentle rocking of the train and the clatter of wheels on the tracks lulled me into a trance and held me there until we reached Fischbach.

CHAPTER 16

A Change in Plans

Returning to visit Fischbach was not the same. In just the few months that Elga and I had been in Munich, many of our friends had moved on. Smaller camps were closing, and when they did, refugees who hadn't yet emigrated were taken into the larger camps. The IRO planned to stop all relocation efforts by June 1950. It was less than 10 months away. Father continued working with the agency toward resettlement, but our family still had no definite prospects.

During the break from my training, I tried to unwind, but Mother's and Father's anxiety about our emigration weighed heavily in the air. We were a family of six, and sponsorships for larger families were challenging to obtain. My parents had explored opportunities in Great Britain, Australia, and Canada.

More recently, refugees were being accepted into the United States. Many Eastern European refugees had obtained sponsorships and employment in the central part of America.

However, like Karlis, most of the jobs were on farms in the Midwest or the cotton fields of Texas. Our family connection in Brazil provided a better possibility. In December, Father would re-apply for visas to Brazil following Elga's and my completion of our training in Munich.

With few friends remaining at Fischbach and too much time on my hands, my thoughts often drifted back to Karlis. I fondly recalled our time together in Munich and how much we enjoyed each other's company. In Germany, the trains ran efficiently carrying the mail. A few days following our evening in Augsburg, a letter arrived from Karlis. He continued to profess his love for me and pleaded for an affirmative answer. I thought more seriously about his proposal and wrote back.

In my letter, I spoke about my uncertainty and fear that I had only been a temporary companion for him in Munich. He wrote back, assuring me his feelings were heartfelt and genuine. We continued corresponding, and through our letters, my feelings grew stronger. I longed to see him again and wondered how or when it could happen.

My time off in Fischbach came to an end. Elga and I needed to return to Munich. It was the beginning of September, and I was ready to go back. I hoped work would provide a needed distraction from the thoughts and concerns swirling through my head. I took a new position in hospital admissions. Unlike Elga, I had never been drawn to the nursing profession and felt a different job would give me a new focus and bring a welcome change.

A few days after our return, a special delivery letter arrived for us from Mother. Knowing it was important, Elga tore it open. I crowded in next to her, and we scanned it together. The one-page message from Mother said that the Brazilian consulate had contacted them. There were medical laboratory positions for our parents in Rio de Janeiro. If they were interested, our family would need to report to a relocation camp to update our interviews and health screenings for visas.

Clutching the letter in her hand, Elga waved it over her head.

"This is wonderful! Father and Mother have been so worried about our resettlement."

"I'm happy for them," I said, my throat tightening and tears welling in my eyes, "but what about Karlis and me?"

Elga stopped short and put her arms around me.

"Oh, Biruta," she said. "I'm sorry. I was so excited about the news. I didn't even think about the two of you. I'm sure something can be worked out."

That night, I went to bed and couldn't sleep. I tossed and turned, thinking about what this meant for me. If I went with my family to Brazil, how could Karlis and I possibly further our relationship? From every angle, it seemed impossible.

I realized that I needed to tell Karlis about this new development. I threw off my bed covers and got up to write him a letter. I hoped he might have an answer and would know what to do. In the morning, I sent the letter. Before long, I received Karlis' reply.

My Dearest Biruta,

Although our future is uncertain, I have my education, and I can make a life for us in the United States. I love you and promise to take care of you. Marry me now, and we can go together to America.

All my love,
Karlis

My heart raced and I became light-headed, reading his words. I hadn't considered an immediate wedding. Yet, I knew I would risk a life without my family to have a life with Karlis. Smiling and clutching his letter to my heart, I spun around in place. Karlis had come up with an unexpected and welcomed solution.

In his letter, he also said that he had written to my parents. He had asked their permission to marry me at the earliest opportunity. He also made inquiries at the American consulate regarding work for the rest of my family in the United States. With my hand trembling, I grabbed a pen to reply to Karlis.

"I'm so moved by your caring concern for not only for me but also for my family. How can I say 'no' to someone who has such a big heart? Of course, I will marry you!"

With a bounce in my step, I hurried to mail my letter. That night, I tucked Karlis' letter under my pillow and slept well.

A few days later, another letter from Karlis arrived.

My Dearest Biruta,

I'm happy beyond all words in your reply! But I have even more good news. I've been working with a liaison officer at the American consulate. He has found an opportunity for your family in the United States!

The liaison has a contact with a Lutheran church in Yankton, South Dakota. They are willing to sponsor a refugee family. In the same city, there is also a state mental health facility with current job openings. There is a good possibility that your parents, as well as you and Elga, can work there. This may be the answer to our prayers for all of us to go to America!

I miss you dearly and can't wait to see you again —
perhaps to get married?

All my love,
Karlis

My heart pounded as I finished reading the letter. Karlis found an alternative for my family other than Brazil! I hoped he had notified Father and Mother about the news.

The next day, a letter came for Elga and me from Father and Mother. After Karlis' inquiry at the American consulate, the IRO had contacted my parents directly. There was employment for the four of us at the state hospital in South Dakota. The Lutheran church agreed to sponsor our family. They'd pay our passage to the United States, and we'd later repay them from our salaries. The Lutheran welfare agency and the church would work together to find our family a place to live and help settle us into our new community.

Elga and I re-read the letter several times, passing it back and forth between us to confirm the words on the page and our family's good fortune.

"Can you believe this? Are you reading what I'm reading?" I asked Elga as she looked at the letter again.

"It looks like Karlis has paved our way to America!" she exclaimed.

As the words sank in, I grabbed Elga in a hug.

"We have jobs and sponsors in the United States!"

Through subsequent letters, Karlis and I changed our plans to marry right away. If we married now, altering his emigration paperwork to include me as his wife, would create delays. It made more sense for me to emigrate with my family and marry when we were all together in America. Karlis and I would then start our new lives together.

With plans to go to the United States, Elga and I were anxious to know more about the country that would become our new home. We had taken English classes since primary school in Riga and continued them in high school at Fischbach. However, most of what we knew about America was from the newsreels at the movies.

The United States government maintained several "American Houses" in the major German cities, including Munich. The houses provided language classes and information about United States culture, history, and politics to assist refugees in becoming more familiar with the country. Wanting to learn more about America, Elga and I took advantage of the resources after our work at the hospital.

❧

At the end of October, Elga and I had a final weekend break from our training and planned to return to visit our family in Fischbach again. Karlis decided to come there at that same time to see me. He had never met Father, Oma, and Maija before. I was anxious for him to meet the rest of the family.

I hadn't seen Karlis since his proposal to me at the end of August at Alfred's DP camp. Our only communication over the past two months had been through our letters. So much had transpired since then. I couldn't wait to see and talk to him again.

The day of our meeting in Fischbach seemed like it would never arrive. Karlis completed his requirements for medical school and had gotten a job at the Augustdorf DP hospital.

He had moved to that camp an hour east of Munster. He was still waiting to be called to a resettlement camp before leaving for America.

On our agreed weekend, Elga and I left Munich and took the train to Fischbach. I stayed at the station waiting for Karlis' train to arrive while Elga went to our family home. I jumped at the sound of every approaching train. When it finally appeared, I stood on tip-toe on the platform, searching the train exits for his familiar profile. I saw him and ran into his arms. He kissed me as deeply as when he had first proposed.

"Hello, future American wife," Karlis said.

Blushing, I replied, "Hello, future American husband."

Both of us beamed as we left the station. We strolled arm-in-arm the short distance to Camp Fischbach.

"My parents were impressed by your letter asking for their permission to marry me. An unexpected bonus was your ability to make connections for the rest of my family to go to America."

"It was mostly good fortune," Karlis replied. "I was desperate. I couldn't let you slip through my fingers. When I got your letter telling me you and your family might be leaving for Brazil, I needed to act quickly. I had to convince your parents to allow me to marry you and then find a way for us all to be together in America."

"You were very persuasive. My parents are completely charmed by you. I can't thank you enough for what you've done for us," I said.

"Anything to keep you in my grasp, my dear," Karlis said, bowing toward me.

"You did seem very eager to ship me off to America with my family, though, and putting off our marriage," I said, pretending to be angry.

"You know it wasn't my intention," Karlis said. "I was just looking for the most expedient way for all of us to get to the United States."

"Okay, I'll forgive you," I said, brushing his cheek with a kiss. "Anyway, we're here," I said as I reached to open the door to my parents' home.

Mother had gotten to know Karlis well during their two-week seminar together in Munich. She told Father and Oma much about him. Karlis' letters to them had also put him in good standing. Father and Oma were eager to meet him. I was thrilled that everyone was happy about our engagement.

Father and Karlis hit it off as soon as they met. Their shared patriotism for Latvia, their mutual medical school experiences at the University in Riga, and their work as physicians at their respective DP camps drew a bond between them. They were both eager to learn about medicine in the United States, as well. Oma watched the two men as they talked animatedly and pulled me aside.

"Karlis is very intelligent and so handsome. His eyes tell me you can certainly trust him," she said. I smiled at her approval of him.

Later, I took Karlis away from my family to walk around Camp Fischbach. I had spent the last four years of my life here and had only been away in Munich for five months. Still, as I saw the camp, I felt sad. I saw the evidence of shuttered barracks and remembered the friends who had left. Sapped of its former life, it felt deserted. We wandered outside the camp to the Gasthaus on the other side of the forest. We went beyond it to Dutzendteich, my classmates' former summer hangout, before returning to camp.

"You know," I said to Karlis, turning to look at the surroundings, "when I first got to Fischbach, I hated it. I was only 15 and thought I could never survive it. Over the years, things did improve. I made many friends here."

Stopping to look at Karlis, and feeling a wave of nostalgia, I asked, "Do you miss Latvia? Do you think we'll ever be able to go back? My childhood in Riga was so idyllic. It seems like such a distant memory."

"I think about my family in Latvia often. Except for Alfreds, and my sister, Zelma, who visited here briefly, I haven't seen any of them since I was drafted by the German army six years ago. I'd like to know that they're all doing well," Karlis said, looking sadly off into the distance.

After a moment, he broke from his thoughts and continued, "I'm not sure if we'll ever be able to go back. Stalin's actions certainly don't bode well. It depends on what, if any, freedoms the Soviets will allow."

Karlis continued to look at me and smiled, "But I'm sure of one thing. I'm glad I found you."

He leaned down to kiss me. The kiss warmed me to my core despite the chill in the air. We continued walking, talking about our future. We took our time returning to my family.

After dinner that evening, Karlis and my family talked about our lives in Latvia. We recalled our past and imagined the opportunities in America. The evening was getting late, but before we retired, Father stood up to address Karlis, poured us all some wine and proposed a toast.

"Karlis, you have been a godsend to Biruta and us. She has found a good man for a husband," Father smiled at him and said, "or should I say, you found her."

Karlis had told my family how he had first noticed me from the streetcar in my green raincoat and umbrella.

Father chuckled and went on, "We are not only gaining a new son-in-law but a new home in America. We are eternally grateful and are proud to give our blessing to this marriage. And what do you say to that, Biruta?" Father asked.

I turned to Karlis, gazing into his eyes, and said, "I've already told him, yes!"

Father raised his glass.

"After the war, our family hoped to return to Riga. Instead, we have remained in Germany these past four years. We remember Opa and all the other family members who couldn't finish the journey. We also pray for the health and safety of our fellow countrymen who remain in Latvia."

I turned to see Karlis brushing the corner of his eye.

Father continued, "To the happy couple and all of us, safe passage to America to start our new lives."

We all raised our glasses to drink.

"On this happy occasion, I also want to share the letter I received from the pastor at our sponsoring church in Yankton," Father said, taking out the letter from his breast coat pocket and giving it to Mother.

She took it from him to read aloud to us in Latvian, translating it from the English.

Dear Dr. Hermanis Riesbergs and family,

I'm happy to inform you that Trinity Lutheran Church in Yankton, South Dakota, is offering to sponsor you and your family in your relocation to the United States.

In addition, we've been assured that full-time positions await you, your wife, and two daughters as psychiatric aides at the South Dakota State Hospital in Yankton. Your employment will begin on or about June 1, 1950, at a salary of $120.00 each per month.

Further information about travel arrangements will be sent to you in the coming weeks. We look forward to meeting all of you and welcoming you to America.

Warm regards for your safe passage,
Rev. Abrahamson, pastor
Trinity Lutheran Church
Yankton, South Dakota

I glanced over and saw tears in Oma's eyes. I'm sure they were tears of happiness for our family, but also tears of sorrow that Opa would not be with us. Mother folded the letter and gave it back to Father. Everyone's eyes in the room glistened with hopes and dreams for our futures.

Breaking the solemn mood in the room, Maija, who was now five, jumped up and down, clapping her hands.

"A hundred and twenty dollars! Is that a lot?" she asked.

An uneasy wave of laughter swept through the room.

Smiling, Mother answered her, "No, dear, it's not a lot, but it's not a little either."

"Can we live on that in America?" Elga asked.

"I'm sure it's just to start," Father replied.

He went on to explain we would be receiving other benefits such as paid vacations and meals at the hospital.

"I'm sure we'll be better compensated once we get established," he said.

"Probably better than anyone can make as a farmhand," I whispered, elbowing Karlis.

The weekend came to an end. Karlis needed to return to his job in Augustdorf. Elga and I needed to return to Munich to finish our last few weeks of training. The three of us said our good-byes to my family and walked to the train station. Karlis and I lingered on the platform until his train arrived.

It had been a wonderful weekend with Karlis and my family. It was hard saying good-bye again. Making it worse, it was unclear when Karlis and I would see each other again. Who would be called first to a relocation camp for emigration processing was uncertain, Karlis, or my family. It could happen soon, or we could all wait for months until all the paperwork hurdles were jumped.

❧

Later in October, Mother wrote to Elga and me that Camp Fischbach was closing. Since my parents had pending immigration plans, they would be allowed to stay, but ultimately, they would also have to move. Later, they were assigned to DP facilities northwest of Nuremberg and moved into a three-story apartment building in the town of Wurzburg. Father and Mother would work at the DP hospital there until our family was called for resettlement processing again.

A few weeks later, I received a brief note from Karlis.

My Dearest Biruta,

> *It was wonderful to see you again in Fischbach and feel the gracious acceptance of your family. It's been*

several weeks since we were together, and it's been too long.
I miss you terribly. However, I have good news!
Over the holidays, I have time off from work.

  Please come to see me for Christmas in Augustdorf.
You can have my room while I stay at the hospital.
I want and need to see you again.

  All my love,
  Karlis

I would complete my training before Christmas and had no other plans other than to join my family in Wurzburg. My heart skipped a beat at the thought of seeing Karlis again. There was no question in my mind I would go to see him in Augustdorf. Christmas couldn't come soon enough.

CHAPTER 17

Christmas in Augustdorf | December 1949

B y mid-December, I completed my nurses' aide training in Munich. Elga and I put off any additional plans for college until after we emigrated to America. As it was, Father and Mother worried we wouldn't be free to go to a relocation camp if our family was called. We obtained our certifications and moved to Wurzburg to wait for notification with our family. Our parents were relieved and happy to have us back with them.

In Wurzburg, Elga and I took a typing course to fill our days and add to our employment skills. We hadn't completed the classes before both of us secured full-time jobs. Elga commuted across town to work at a local hospital, while I got a secretarial job at the IRO offices. My job paid better than Elga's and I had better hours. I quietly delighted in knowing it.

Planning for my visit to see Karlis, I agonized about what to wear. I deliberated over which dresses to pack and only made my final decisions the night before. I hardly slept thinking about seeing Karlis again.

The next morning, I got up before the sun rose and re-checked what I had packed. I put on a dress that I thought best flattered my features and checked myself in the mirror. Elga stirred in her bed and looked at me with one eye open. She smiled, nodding her approval, and went back to sleep. Grabbing my bag, I went into my parents' room to wish them a "Merry Christmas." I hugged them and ran out the door for the train station. I didn't want to be late.

I reached the station on time and climbed aboard. The trip north would take several hours. By mid-morning, it already felt like the longest day of my life. German trains ran efficiently, but today it crawled along. The train made several stops between Wurzburg and Augustdorf, lingering at each station. Why were there so many stops?

In the late afternoon, the train finally pulled into Augustdorf. I looked out the windows, searching the platform for Karlis and didn't see him. I frowned as I gathered my bag and headed for the exit. On the platform, I still didn't see him.

I waited a few minutes outside the station, but it was December, and the weather was brisk. I saw a small, run-down coffee shop with a few tables inside next to the newspaper stand. At least the coffee shop would be warmer, and I decided to go inside. Karlis couldn't have forgotten the date or time of my arrival. He had written so passionately about looking forward to seeing me again. I ordered some coffee and sat down by the window facing the platform.

A few minutes later, a figure rushed by the coffee shop window and stopped to watch my train leaving the station. It was Karlis. He whirled around, his eyes searching the platform.

He finally saw me sitting in the coffee shop window and ran inside. Breathless, he rushed over to plant a kiss on my cheek.

"Forgive me, Biruta. I'm so sorry. I was getting your Christmas present and was delayed. I placed my order weeks ago, but the shop was busy with last-minute customers."

He placed a small package wrapped in silver foil into my hands.

"I hope this will make it up to you."

I smiled, standing up to give Karlis a warm hug.

"I was afraid for a moment you might have forgotten about me," I teased as I sat back down to unwrap the gift and gently lifted the lid of a small delicate box. Inside was a traditional Latvian amber and silver brooch.

"Oh, Karlis! It's lovely. Where on earth did you find this?"

"There is a Latvian jeweler at my camp. He's an artisan from Riga. I had him make it especially for you to remind you of home."

I ran my fingers over the smooth amber stone and touched the delicate metal tassels hanging from the pin.

"It's so thoughtful of you and so beautiful," I sighed, admiring it.

I pinned it on and grinned across the table.

"You had me worried when I didn't see you at the station. I thought you might have changed your mind about our Christmas together."

Karlis stood up and came around the table to gather me to my feet. Holding me close, he whispered in my ear, "How could I change my mind? I've been waiting to see you again ever since I last saw you."

The customers warming themselves with their coffee and the shop keeper wiping the counter looked up to take notice.

"Karlis, everyone is staring at us!"

"Who cares?" he said and turned to address the people in the coffee shop.

"This is our first Christmas together, and she's going to marry me!"

People smiled, and a few came over to congratulate us.

"Merry Christmas and God bless both of you!" they said and returned to their tables.

"Let's sit down," I said, "I have something for you as well." I handed him my present.

During our time together in Munich, Karlis had admired the fine German porcelains we had seen in some of the shops. I had set aside some money from my first few paychecks to purchase a small glazed royal blue plate, rimmed in gold. The Holy Family, centered in the scene, was painted in ethereal white outlines. A beam of light poured down upon Mother and Child with gold stars shining in the background.

"I wanted this as a reminder of our first Christmas together," I said, as Karlis gingerly unwrapped and held the delicate plate.

"I've never seen a more beautiful Christmas scene. It's truly a work of art. I will treasure this gift and always remember this day," he said as he reached across the table and squeezed my hand.

Carefully re-wrapping the plate, he said, "But the afternoon is getting late. Let's get you settled in my room."

Grabbing my suitcase and his gift, Karlis and I took a short taxi ride to his camp.

⤛⤜

Much like Fischbach, Augustorf DP camp was also a former army base. His room was simple and small; a bed, a small table, and a desk and chair facing the window. I unpacked a few items. Then we went to the camp dining hall to grab a bite to eat.

Since it was Christmas Eve, we decided to attend late services at the camp church. We walked arm-in-arm across the grounds, our footsteps crunching on the thin crust of snow. It was a brisk, clear evening. As was my habit, I looked up at the stars in the night sky and smiled.

We entered the church and saw a candlelit tree. It was just like the ones I remembered from childhood. It glimmered behind the altar giving off the same piney scent. An organ played familiar Christmas carols in the background, reminding me of my family gathered around Mother at the piano at Alexander Heights. This was my first Christmas away from my family. I wondered what they might be doing at this moment.

I looked up at Karlis with my arm still threaded through his. His smile radiated down to me. Though I missed my family, tonight, I was happy to be with Karlis.

When the church service ended, we didn't say a word as we left the church and walked back towards Karlis' room. We didn't want to disturb the mood of this special evening,

We reached Karlis' room and entered. Moonlight streamed through the window, dimly lighting the room. Disregarding the lights, Karlis lit a single candle. The flame flickered and danced, casting shadows on the wall. He turned on the radio as we sat down side-by-side on the edge of the bed. He wrapped his arm around my shoulders. I leaned in, nestling under his arm.

We sat for a time listening to Christmas carols on the radio. At midnight, the radio announcer reported the tolling of the Christmas bells around Europe: the Berlin Cathedral; St. Peter's in Rome; Notre Dame in Paris; and, St. Paul's in

London. All was calm, and all was bright. No more bombs were dropping this Christmas Eve. For the time being, there was "Peace on Earth".

"You look so far away," Karlis said. "What are you thinking?"

I shook my head, "Nothing," I said. "Just how happy I am at this moment."

"Are you sure?"

"Of course, I am," I said. "How about you? What are you thinking?"

"I'm more than happy," he smiled. "But to be truthful, I'm also thinking about my family in Ventspils. I'm wondering how they're doing this Christmas. It's been a long time since I've spent it with the people I love. Tonight I'm blessed to have a beautiful girl sitting next to me who says she'll marry me. Biruta, you're my best Christmas present ever."

He gripped me closer, and we kissed.

I had planned to return to Wurzburg the day after Christmas to be with my family. However, Karlis persuaded me to stay through the New Year. I notified Father and Mother, letting them know my change in plans.

The day after Christmas, Karlis and I took a cab to Detmold, a larger city just a few miles from Augustdorf, to shop for our wedding bands. In the Latvian tradition, wedding rings were purchased when a couple got engaged. The engagement date and names were engraved inside. Couples then wore their rings on their left hand until the wedding day and then switched them to their right hand at the end of the ceremony.

We found the central shopping district and strolled down the streets looking for a jeweler. I was in a playful mood and turned to Karlis.

"We have a problem."

"Oh, and what might that be?" Karlis asked.

"What date do we have engraved inside our rings, the night that you asked me to marry you in Augsburg or when my parents gave us their blessing in Fischbach?" I asked.

"That is a dilemma," he said, "I think it has to be when I asked you in Augsburg. I had a feeling you might say yes."

"Oh, did you? But I didn't say 'yes' then, and it wasn't official until Father and Mother gave us their blessing in Fischbach," I replied, grinning back at him.

"You have a point. I guess October 22, 1949, it will have to be," he said.

We entered the jewelers, picked out a pair of simple gold bands, had them engraved, and placed them on the ring finger of our left hands.

"I hope it won't be too long before we can switch these to our right hands," Karlis said with a gleam in his eye.

We spent the rest of the day having a late lunch and window shopping. Just before leaving, we passed a photography studio.

"Look, let's get our engagement picture taken," I said, pulling Karlis toward the shop.

He agreed, and we went inside to find the photographer sitting behind the counter.

"We've just gotten our wedding rings, and now we'd like an official engagement picture too. Do we need to make an appointment?" Karlis asked.

"No, no need. It's the day after Christmas, and as you can see, I'm not very busy. Can you sit for the picture now?" the photographer asked.

We nodded and followed him back into his studio. He suggested a pose with both of us looking off together in profile. Pleased that he had been able to accommodate us, we left his shop.

The sun was low in the gray winter sky, and a chill returned to the air. We huddled together in the cab, returning to Karlis' camp. I looked at the shiny new band on my right hand, admiring it.

"This has been a productive day. We're two steps closer to making our marriage official. We have our rings, and we've taken our engagement picture. I can't wait to see how they'll turn out," I said.

"I'm not worried. Any picture with you in it will be a masterpiece."

I shook my head at Karlis and gave him a gentle nudge.

During the week, Karlis scheduled activities for us, and the days flew by. One night, we returned to Detmold for dinner and to attend an opera. Karlis was a classical music lover. He could hear the first few notes of a symphony and name the piece and its composer. On a different day, we went sightseeing in the countryside.

On our last evening together, we planned to go to a New Year's Eve party at the camp. It was the start of a new decade, 1950, and it promised to be a joyous occasion. When we arrived, the room was crowded and filled with energy. Aside from Karlis, I knew almost no one, except a few of his friends who I had met earlier in the week.

Many of the people here, like at other DP camps, had pending plans to emigrate and were celebrating their last days in Germany. Karlis navigated the room, back-slapping and wishing well to friends who were leaving. I tagged along behind him, feeling out of place. It was our last night together, and I knew we probably wouldn't see each other again for weeks. I was disappointed and annoyed not to have him all to myself.

Karlis noticed some close colleagues across the room and asked to be excused. I stood alone in the corner of the room as other dancing couples twirled by, and my irritation grew. Suddenly, Karlis reappeared before to me, apologizing for leaving me alone. He grabbed my hand, leading me out on to the dance floor. Once I was in his arms, my resentment melted.

We danced the rest of the evening. At midnight, we embraced and kissed, joining the other couples around us ringing in the New Year. Shortly after, we left the party to enjoy the rest of the evening alone.

In the morning, we took our time going to the station and arrived just in time for me to catch my train back to Wurzburg. Before I boarded, Karlis embraced me, and we kissed. He pulled away to look into my eyes.

"I've had a wonderful week with you. Why is it at the end of our visits, someone is always leaving, and the other is left alone? I can't wait until we can be together endlessly."

My throat tightened, and I was unable to speak. I simply nodded and fought back my tears. It would be some time before we saw each other again, and we promised to write as often as we could.

When the train whistle blew, we kissed one last time. I turned to enter the train. I knew if I looked back at Karlis again, I might break down and cry. Instead, I fumbled toward my seat and sat down. Thinking about our first Christmas together, I reached up to touch the silver brooch on my lapel. I then gazed at the engagement band on my finger, admiring it. A feeling of warmth enveloped me, and I smiled. On the trip back to Wurzburg, I went over the past week, remembering every moment with Karlis.

After my Christmas visit, weeks and months went by, and neither of us heard anything further about our respective resettlement plans. Karlis continued working at the Augusdorf DP hospital and I at the IRO offices while we waited. We wrote to each other almost every day, but I grew impatient. Our jobs and sponsorships for the United States were arranged. We were all waiting to be called to finalize the visas process. What was taking so long?

Karlis wrote to say he had a long weekend coming up, but he was going on an excursion with some of his friends. They wanted to see as much as they could of Germany before emigrating. Initially, I was upset. Why wasn't he coming to see me? Instead, Easter was coming up in mid-April when he had a week-long break. He promised to come to Wurzburg then to see me. It softened my disappointment, and I began counting the days.

As promised, Karlis came at Easter. We had a wonderful time together with my family in Wurzburg or went to Nuremberg for dinner, the movies, or the opera. In no time, the week was over. We found ourselves saying good-bye to each other at the train station again. We could only hope that in the coming weeks, either he or my family would soon be called to a resettlement camp.

In May, a full month later, our family was finally notified. I wrote to Karlis immediately, expecting he had been contacted as well, but he had heard nothing. It was puzzling to me that he was still waiting. Karlis was the first to secure his sponsorship, and through his efforts, our family had obtained ours. Nevertheless, I remained confident that it would only be a matter of days before Karlis would also be notified.

The following week, our family went to the resettlement camp. We went through the process of interviews and screenings again and were cleared for immigration. I thought about all my family had experienced since we had left Riga in June 1944. Now, almost six years later, it was hard to imagine the next chapter of our lives was actually about to begin.

Our tentative departure date was set for some time at the end of May. We would leave from the port of Bremerhaven, Germany, and our family was sent to Grohn, a DP camp closer to the port. Karlis wrote, saying he would come to visit the weekend before we were scheduled to leave for the United States.

On the day of Karlis' arrival, I hurried to the Grohn station. I spotted him getting off the train and maneuvered around the other passengers to get to him unseen, stealing up behind him.

"Meeting like this at train stations is getting awfully old, isn't it?"

Karlis whirled around. "I know, I'd rather be married and see you every day," he said, picking me up and swinging me around before embracing me.

"Karlis, I can't believe you haven't been called to a resettlement camp yet. I wish you were leaving, too," I said, scrunching my face into a pout.

"Yes. I expected it myself," Karlis said, looking down and shaking his head. "but I'm sure it will be soon."

We went to my family's apartment in Grohn. The mood in the household was buoyant. Maija rushed at Karlis as soon as he stepped in the door.

"Karlis, did you hear?" she shouted, running into his arms. "We're going to America!" She nuzzled his shoulder and asked, "Are you coming, too?"

"No, I'm going to have to wait a little while longer, angel. We'll all be together again soon, I promise," he said. "Would that make you happy?"

"Yes, and then you and Biruta are getting married, right?"

"Yes, my little darling," he smiled and then turned around to grin at me.

Karlis had to return to Augustdorf at the end of the weekend. We were leaving each other again. Our only comfort was knowing that the next time we would see each other would be in America. However, the biggest question was when. As always, we promised to write as often as possible. Karlis wanted to hear the details about our journey to America and my first impressions.

Karlis and Biruta, engagement photo, 1949

CHAPTER 18

Leaving Again

Give me your tired, your poor,
your huddled masses yearning to breathe free... [12]

U ntil our family's sailing date was confirmed, I continued to work at the IRO offices in Wurzburg and ran across some staggering figures. There were 1.2 million refugees, like us, who were displaced after the war, needing food, clothing, shelter, and resettlement services. The sheer numbers gave me a perspective of why our emigration process had taken so long.

In the paperwork, I also found out how our family was getting to America. On our departure date, two ships, the *General Stewart* and the *General Sturgis*, would be sailing from Bremerhaven, Germany to New York City. Both ships were U.S. Army transports (USATs) during the war. In 1946, they carried military troops back from Japan. They were decommissioned, rebuilt, and re-commissioned for the IRO to transport thousands of refugees to different parts of the world.

In 1948, the *General Stewart* and the *General Sturgis* were a part of the fleet of 40 ships that made 150 sailings taking refugees to Australia. Between April 1949 and April 1950, refugees were also taken to the United States, Argentina, Brazil, Venezuela, and Canada.

Our family was assigned to the *General Stewart*. We, along with 800 other refugees, would take an eight-day voyage across the Atlantic Ocean to America. We packed all that we had in crates and made last-minute purchases. Then we checked and re-checked our bags. This was it. Once we left, we wouldn't have the opportunity to return.

Elga and I volunteered to be part of an advance unit. Around 120 staff would assist in organizing and readying the ships for their passengers. On May 29, 1950, we arose early from Grohn resettlement camp and left to go to the *General Stewart*. We would reunite with our family on the ship in a few days.

The advance unit was organized into groups. Elga was assigned to a nursing unit and me to a secretarial pool. At camp, we loaded onto trucks to go to the train station. From there, we took the train to Bremerhaven, our departure port, and arrived two hours later. There, two large gray military vessels were docked side-by-side in the harbor. These were the two ships, the *General Stewart* and the *General Sturgis*, that we would be taking us to America.

Elga and I separated at boarding. We had different duties and went to our respective job locations. During a break, we were shown our sleeping quarters and met up again. Fifty women were assigned bunks in one large room. We rolled our eyes at each other. It reminded us of our voyage to Danzig and the barracks at Camp Fischbach. Later, we learned 200 men were assigned to one area and considered ourselves lucky.

I returned to work and finished my typing tasks early. Some other women from my unit decided to explore the ship, and I joined them. We found a lounge on the top deck comfortably furnished with cozy overstuffed chairs and a piano. On the bookshelves were books, games, and cards. In one corner, we found a card table and chairs and started a card game. We talked and decided the area would be perfect for holding a dance in the evening for the advance unit. The idea was not a success. There weren't enough women in the group, the men were horrible dancers, and the accordionist was in a foul mood — not a great way to start the week.

We completed our advance preparations for the sailing, and four days later, I wrote to Karlis.

June 1, 1950
Dearest Karlis,

Today, the train with the passengers for the General Sturgis arrived. The ship was docked next to us. We finished our work quickly to go to the top levels and watch the people board. Soon their deck was completely filled.

By mid-afternoon, the General Sturgis blasted its horn, signaling its departure. Everyone on both ships waved white handkerchiefs at each other. Across the water, I even saw the mother of one of my friends. It was a sight to behold.

Tugboats came to push, then pull and turn the General Sturgis away from the dock and out into open water. The ship got smaller and smaller as it went out to sea and vanished from sight. In no time, the General Stewart sat alone at the dock. The same tugs would soon come to steer us away from the pier and out to sea as well. My heart fell as I realized that I, too, would soon be saying good-bye to Europe.

All my love,
Biruta

The train with passengers for the *General Stewart* arrived soon after. I saw Father, Mother, Oma, and Maija board and waved to them. Elga and I joined them as they settled in. Our ship was scheduled to leave that evening. However, there were unknown delays, and the *General Stewart* still sat at the dock in the evening. Elga and I returned to our bunks for the night, but in bed, my mind raced. I was excited about leaving yet worried about Karlis and our family's permanent departure from Europe. I tossed and turned for some time before falling asleep.

☙

It was a full 24 hours later before our ship got underway. As the port faded from view, I looked out on the water and thought I might get seasick. I heard the best remedy for it was not to think about it. So, I focused my thoughts on the chugging pulse of the ship's engines. It distracted my thoughts, and my seasickness never came. That night, there was thunder, but the following day was pleasant. Later, I overheard some sailors predicting pleasant sailing with calm waters. I was happy to hear it.

In the afternoon, we passed the shores of England. Seagulls followed us for a time, and I saw fishing boats and other ships.

Soon, the last specks of land that we would see for days melted into the horizon. I said my final farewell to Europe. All my life, I had lived my life surrounded by earthen tones. Now the world I saw before me was only in varying shades of blue and gray.

We left the Baltic Sea and entered the Atlantic Ocean, where the swells were more noticeable. I had work to do in the ship's office. It was near the front of the vessel and pitched considerably. After a half-hour of trying to work, a co-worker and I decided it wasn't worth the suffering and went to get some fresh air.

We went outside to the middle of the ship, where the swaying wasn't as severe. It was a sunny afternoon, and I became mesmerized by the waves and saw dolphins jumping alongside us in the water. Until my co-worker and I got our sea legs, we decided to spend the rest of the day recovering out on the deck.

We were well taken care of during our voyage. For breakfast, we had eggs. In the evening, we were often served chicken dinners followed by ice cream for dessert. Some people said the portions were too small. Others didn't eat, in case they lost it to the sea. There were many jokes about feeding the fishes, but only those that didn't get seasick laughed. We were also issued PX cards to go shopping for chocolates or fruit juices or personal items of our choosing.

Eight days later, I wrote to Karlis about my experiences on the ship and the highlight of arriving in New York harbor.

June 9, 1950
Dearest Karlis,

The weather at sea was pleasant and, as a result, we made good time during our crossing. A rumor went around that the General Stewart was one of the fastest ships at sea and that we had already passed the General Sturgis.

Still, there was a request from the authorities to slow
our passage and arrive a day later. Many were upset
by the news. Finally, toward dusk, our ship approached the
New York harbor, and outlines of tall buildings emerged
on the horizon.

The ship wasn't allowed entry into the port for the
evening. We were at anchor and couldn't disembark
until morning. People went on the upper decks to watch
the glimmering lights from the city. Automobiles looked
like small bugs in the distance, speeding along the shoreline
drives with lights glowing in a steady stream — a pretty
sight in the fading sunlight. Spotlights were shining
on the Statue of Liberty.

It was a very emotional sight.

All my love,
Biruta

On June 10, 1950, we were up at 5:00 a.m. to disembark. And what did we find? A hot stinking entry into the city with no fresh air anywhere. After days at sea, I should've been happy to greet our new home, but instead, I felt sad that we had said good-bye to Europe. Suddenly, I was afraid to touch the solid ground beneath my feet in this strange land.

America was not what I imagined it to be. When we went through customs, our German camera was inspected and confiscated. We saw very little of New York City because the trains ran underground. There were no streetcars like the ones in Riga. The only parts of the city we saw were on our way to the train station. Some of the streets looked terrible with old fashioned, quaint stores. I preferred the New York

I had seen at a distance on our first night in the harbor; the Statue of Liberty lit up at night and the twinkling lights of the skyscrapers and cars.

Once through customs, the members from the Lutheran Welfare organization were there to greet us and provide train tickets to Sioux City, Iowa. We were given six dollars apiece for food during the two-day trip and taken to Grand Central Station.

I entered the station, and my impressions of America changed. My jaw dropped at seeing the marble floors, the glass chandeliers, and bronze and stone carvings inside. It looked more like a museum than a train station. It was truly amazing and grand. I didn't want to look uncivilized with my mouth hanging open, so I pretended it was all to be expected.

Our family boarded the train to Chicago. A few days later, I penned a letter to Karlis about our trip.

June 12, 1950
Dearest Karlis,

Our train trip to the Midwest began in the afternoon in a wonderfully comfortable train. When we started, there were two rail cars full of Displaced Persons, but people were dropped off along the route, and the cars soon emptied.

We slept overnight on the train and arrived in Chicago the next morning. Everyone got out to change trains. We were now seven hours behind Europe and moved our watches back for the last time. We boarded for Sioux City in an even more comfortable train.

*The trip was wonderful. The countryside was exactly
as we had seen in American magazines; the wooden
farmhouses painted white, and barns and other
structures around them painted red. In the small towns
and suburbs, the houses were surrounded by trees and
green lawns with no fences!*

*We've been on the train for two days and must have
seen half of America. Though tired, I'm enjoying the
experience. Who knows when we will travel this way again.*

All my love,
Biruta

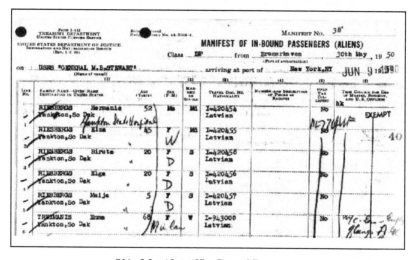

Ship Manifest of In-Bound Passengers

The Displaced Persons Commission welcomes you to the United States of America.

The Congress of the United States of America has established the Displaced Persons Commission to select for immigration to this country, persons displaced as a result of World War II. Under the principles laid down by the Congress, you are among those selected.

The Congress is interested in how displaced persons fare after settling in the United States. So that the Congress may be kept informed on this matter, it requires that each person who immigrated to the United States as the head of a family or as a single person provide certain factual information.

The information is to be provided twice a year, for two years. The reporting dates are July 1 and January 1. The first report is required on the next reporting date after you have been in the country 60 or more days. Each of the reports must be in the mails to reach us by the date specified, but may be mailed as much as fifteen days earlier.

The form for reporting is provided by the Displaced Persons Commission. The form to be used will be available on May 15 for the July 1 report and on November 15 for the January 1 report. It will be available at local offices of the U. S. Immigration and Naturalization Service.

The Displaced Persons Commission wishes you every success in your new life in the United States of America.

Sincerely,

Ugo Carusi, Chairman

Edward M. O'Connor

Harry N. Rosenfield

U.S. Welcome Letter and Train Tickets from New York City to Sioux City, Iowa

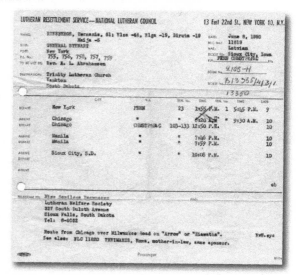

233

CHAPTER 19

Letters from Yankton | June - August 1950

W hen our train arrived in Sioux City, Iowa, no one was there to greet us. For several minutes the six of us, Oma, Father, Mother, Elga, Maija, and I stood in the train station in a daze. We were tired, hungry, and rumpled from eight days of crossing the Atlantic and two days of traveling on a train. Whoever saw us must have wondered from what corner of the earth we had fallen. To make matters worse, our English was limited.

Oma wrung hands and lamented, "Oh, dear. No one is here for us. Now what?"

"I have the church's contact information," Mother said, rummaging through her purse. "My English is passable. I'll call them."

She found a pay phone at the station. When she returned, we all turned to her for an explanation.

"The Lutheran Welfare agency gave the church in Yankton an incorrect date. They're not expecting us until tomorrow."

Father, sitting on a station bench, rose to his feet.

"We know no one here and have no resources. What are we to do? We had only enough money for food on the train."

Mother put her hand on Father's shoulder. "It's alright, Hermanis. Fortunately, they told me a church member is doing business here today," she said. "He's being notified and will come to get us. We're instructed to wait for him here."

The minutes ticked by as Father paced. Oma and Mother tried to entertain Maija while Elga and I looked around the station, gathering clues about our new home. We were truly strangers in a strange land.

About an hour later, a well-dressed gentleman in a suit arrived at the station. He was very kind and apologetic. Through gestures and short phrases, Mother was able to understand that he only had a small car and couldn't transport us to Yankton with our belongings. He made a few phone calls and came back to tell us we would be staying at a hotel for the night. Someone would come to get us in the morning. We crammed ourselves into his car for the short ride to the hotel.

The man purchased meals for us at a restaurant nearby. While we ate, he took our baggage and talked to the hotel clerk next door. A few minutes later, he returned saying everything had been arranged. We finished our meals, walked to the hotel, and the man left.

At the desk, the clerk gave Father three keys. With a puzzled look, Father showed them to Mother. She asked the clerk why we had been given three keys. He replied that since there were six of us, three rooms had been paid for, two people per room. We looked at each other in disbelief. On the ship, we had slept in tiered bunks with a room full of people. On the train, we had slept in our seats. This would be a luxury!

Exhausted from the entire ordeal, we were anxious to get to our rooms. We followed the clerk through a pleasantly decorated, carpeted hallway to three numbered doors next to each other. The clerk opened one of them, and we followed him inside. The soft carpeting from the hall spilled into the room with a full-size bed at its center. Toward the window was a small desk and chair. My parents nodded their approval, and the clerk left. We inspected the room further, checking the bed and smoothing our hands over the starched white sheets and the soft fluffy pillows.

Maija bounced from the chair to the bed and stopped to notice two doors in the room. Running to one, she opened it to find an empty closet with hangers for our clothes. She opened the second door, and we all gasped. It was a private bathroom with a sink, tub, and toilet. It included a small set of toiletries and fresh, clean towels.

"Praise God for the kindness of our church sponsors!" Oma exclaimed.

Elga grabbed a key from Father. I followed her out to the hall while Oma took Maija to the third room. Elga opened the adjacent room and rushed in.

"It's exactly the same, and it has its own bathroom, too!" I shouted back to Father and Mother.

"Ours too!" Oma confirmed. "We'll sleep well for our first night in America."

"I'm taking my bath first!" Elga exclaimed.

When it was my turn, I stepped into the warm, welcoming water and soaked with my eyes closed. With stomach filled and relaxed from my bath, fatigue set in. Elga and I got ready for bed and crawled in, squirming under the crisp, clean sheets and hugging our pillows. I fell asleep wondering what other new surprises would greet us in the morning.

Early on Sunday, June 11, 1950, two cars picked us up at the hotel in Sioux City. We'd be taken 60 miles to Yankton, South Dakota, to begin our first day at Trinity Lutheran, our sponsoring church.

"Starting our first day in America at our new hometown church has got to be a good omen," Oma said and smiled.

The cars pulled up to the church shortly before Reverend Abrahamson was to start his Sunday service. We were unable to talk to him for long. Instead, our family was ushered to the front row pew of the church like royalty. People stared as we filed in.

Once we were seated and the service began, I focused my attention on the English words to see how much I understood. After the sermon and last hymn, the Reverend asked our family to stand. He introduced us as the new refugee family the church was sponsoring and explained to the congregation how we had come to Yankton. He then urged the parishioners to assist us in any way that they could. The service ended, and our family was ushered outside to the church courtyard.

Standing next to Father, Mother whispered, "This is awful! It's awkward enough to be singled out in front of the entire congregation, but for the Reverend to ask them to help us like we're beggars is humiliating!"

"Yes, we don't expect charity," Father replied. "We're educated people with promised jobs."

Oma interrupted, "I'm not sure that's what the Reverend intended. He was just encouraging the parishioners to lend us a helping hand. After all the hardships we've endured, I think we can accept it graciously."

As church members filed out, people came up to our family to shake our hands and welcome us to the community. Oma smiled at them and then looked back at Father and Mother knowingly.

Afterward, we were taken to Reverend Abrahamson's and his wife's home. We would be staying with them and other church members until we had an apartment of our own. The Abrahamsons invited us to join them for a simple breakfast of cornflakes and toast.

During better times in Latvia, breakfasts were one of the more substantial meals of the day. A typical breakfast consisted of cured meats, smoked fish, eggs, cheese, tomatoes, and other cold vegetables along with a variety of breads. America was described as the land of plenty, and I expected similar. Afterward, I pulled Elga aside. She agreed when I said it had been a strange breakfast and that they must have eaten something better earlier.

Later that afternoon, people from the church came over to the Reverend's home to get to know our family. Even though conversations were labored, everyone's willingness to help was apparent. The people were courteous and friendly, not the snobbish Americans we had heard about.

Struggling through the language barrier made it a strenuous afternoon. We were still recovering from our journey. By early evening, our family was drained and went to bed. In the morning, we joined the Abrahamsons again for breakfast. It was the same menu of cornflakes and toast. Even breakfasts in America were different.

After we had eaten, Reverend Abrahamson showed us a map of the United States. The two-day journey from New York had taken us only halfway through the northcentral part of America. He offered to drive the family around the local countryside to get a better feel for the area we would now call home.

Driving west of town, Reverend Abrahamson talked about the state's geography and history. Mother translated the information in Latvian to Father, Oma, and Maija as we drove. Yankton, a city of about 7,700 people, sat on the northern banks of the Missouri River in southeastern South Dakota. The river formed a border with the state's southern neighbor, Nebraska. The Reverend pointed its banks on the opposite shore.

Turning north, we saw miles of rolling hills of wheat and corn fields covering the landscape. There were few trees, and the horizon could be seen in all directions. I thought about the forests around Mezparks and asked Reverend Abrahamson what everyone did here for Christmas trees. He said they were brought in from Minnesota. He added that even more vast stretches of flatlands, called prairies, were located in the western part of the state. Horses, cattle, and buffalo grazed there on open ranges of land.

When Mother repeated the information to Maija, she asked, "Are there real cowboys and Indians?"

"I think you've heard too many stories, little one," Mother laughed but translated the question back to Reverend Abrahamson.

"It's a fair question. Around here, people wear cowboy hats and boots and tend cattle and horses on the grasslands, but usually, they're referred to as ranchers. Most Indians live on designated lands called reservations."

While learning about the United States, I read that Indians had roamed the plains here just a few hundred years ago. On our drive, many places, including our new hometown, had Indian names. I hadn't seen any native Americans yet and found it strange.

We turned east and drove to Sioux Falls, a city of 53,000 people, the largest city in the state. Reverend Abrahamson told us that a small community of Latvians lived there. Father and

Mother took note of it, looking at each other and smiling. From Sioux Falls, we headed south and west again, returning to Yankton, having made a full circle. We'd been driving the entire morning.

⤳⤙

At first, it was exciting to learn about the area where we would be living, but after just a few days, the novelty was wearing off.

June 13, 1950
Dearest Karlis,

> *The hardest part of being here is moving from place to place. After our first night with the Abrahamsons, we stayed at two different homes with two different families. We're like gypsies, not knowing where we will sleep or eat the next day. Until our family finds a place to call our own, we live like nomads.*
>
> *Parishioners check in on us regularly where we stay, but they don't stay long. They mostly talk with the homeowner while we stand alone.*
>
> *I'm sure it would be the same had we immigrated to Brazil, but it is disheartening, and I wish it were different. It was the same in Germany.*
>
> *Refugees were tolerated but never welcomed. I want to feel like I belong somewhere again. Even so, the church is so gracious; it's really a sin to complain.*
>
> *All my love,*
> *Biruta*

Mother said the elders of the church, especially our sponsors, were our guardian angels. They found us a renovated apartment.

To our sponsors, we said, "Nice!" but it was really nothing special. It was just three small bedrooms, a bathroom, and a kitchen with a refrigerator and a stove. The apartment was upstairs above a liquor store on the corner of one of downtown's busiest streets and was very noisy. Nevertheless, we were tired of spending nights in other people's homes, so we accepted it. I had to admit, compared to the DP camps, the apartment was pure gold.

The apartment was unfurnished, so some church members gave us a bed, a table, and a few chairs. The first night, Mother and Oma slept in the bed while Father, Elga, Maiija, and I slept on the floor. It was the middle of June, and the temperature reached 104 degrees. The apartment didn't cool down much at night. I tossed and turned and didn't sleep well.

A few days later, beds arrived for all of us. For the first time in ages, I slept in my own bed in a place I could call home. I heard that what you dreamt in a new place foretold your future, so I focused on pleasant thoughts before falling asleep.

More home goods were donated. Oma hung curtains and tidied the apartment, adding her own decorating touches. It made it feel more like home. We unpacked our bags and crates and hung clothes in the closets, putting things in their new rightful place. It was a joy after living out of suitcases for weeks. In the morning, a bouquet of peonies arrived at our door.

Elga and I took advantage of a movie theater a few steps from our door. However, listening to the radio in the evenings was our family's primary source of entertainment. Someone from the church donated a radio to us. It helped immensely with our language skills. Our own radio had made the trans-Atlantic voyage from Germany and played as well as it did in Europe. Now, both radios competed.

The first night we plugged in the radios, Maija, who had turned six, stood in front of our old radio with a quizzical look.

"Mommy, before our radio only talked German. How did it learn to speak English so well?"

The entire family burst out laughing. Feeling hurt, Maija pouted. Seeing her upset, Father explained to her in simple terms how a radio worked.

꘎

The following day, Father, Mother, Elga, and I were taken on a tour of the state hospital facilities where we would work. The orientation lasted most of the day. The grounds were spacious, and some patients operated a farm like at Alexander Heights. For recreation, there was even a small golf course for patients and staff. The doctor who showed us the hospital reported hundreds of patients from all over the state were treated here and benefitted greatly.

The first floor in one of the buildings looked impressive with a marble staircase and original paintings on the walls. Father and Mother were taken upstairs to the hospital floors while Elga and I waited. Later, on returning home, our parents reported the wards were very basic but better than at Alexander Heights. Still, seeing where we would be working made me excited to start.

I was exhausted from using English the entire day. Elga felt the same. We understood the written form of the language, but the pronunciation and subtleties were challenging. Mother was the best at speaking English. Father struggled more than Elga and I, while Oma and Maija knew little. Somehow, we needed to adapt. We would start work the following day.

The town of Yankton had no public transportation, and our family had no way of getting around on our own. It was good we lived close to the downtown stores. At issue, however, was how we would get to work at the state hospital almost four miles away. We relied on rides from others or the hospital car if it was available.

We all started work the next day as psychiatric attendants but were assigned different wards. Despite being physicians, Father and Mother were assigned the same job as Elga and me. The doctor in charge promised that in a few weeks, my parents could work as physicians. I wrote to Karlis about our first days at work.

June 16, 1950
Dearest Karlis,

After just a few days at the state hospital, I feel this is not the right job for me. I work on a ward with older women patients, feeding, washing, and dressing them, which requires no special skill from me.

Some days I'm asked to take the patients to the lounge for movies or singing sessions. I'm not sure how it helps them. I can only imagine how demeaning this kind of work is for my parents.

Elga works on a ward with more violent patients. When her patients become aggressive, they are restrained in chairs in the main room.

They're not medicated because there is nothing known to help.

Some of the buildings and furnishings at the hospital are
impressive, but of what benefit are grand pianos, radios,
and record players to those who aren't in touch with their
surroundings? Father says his situation in the men's ward is
the same and is thinking about looking for other work. At first,
Mother is against the idea but then says if he finds another
opportunity, he should take it.

While the four of us work during the day, Oma takes
care of Maija. Oma knows very little English, so she
relies on us for socialization and news of the day. The entrance
to the downtown second-floor apartment is from an outside
stairway. There is just a tiny yard, so they rarely go out.

Little Maija spends most of her days inside the four walls.
To get fresh air, she sits at the bottom of the stairs and looks
at her books. Sometimes she plays in the dirty side streets
with other children, mostly boys. They made a wooden gun
for her with her name scratched in the handle and pretend
to shoot at each other. Who knows if they are cowboys or
Indians? She'll turn into a slum child if school doesn't start
soon, but it's only the beginning of summer.

All my love,
Biruta

As an immigrant, I made some interesting observations. In America, religious affiliations identified many hospitals, colleges, and schools. Elga wanted to complete her nursing degree. Our Lutheran church sponsor wanted her to apply to a Lutheran nursing school 80 miles away, even though there was a Catholic nursing school in town. The same was true for English classes. When Father, Mother, Elga, and I signed up for an evening course taught at a nearby Catholic college, some people from the church didn't like it. Locally, no other classes were available, so we were allowed to attend.

The city newspaper was also peculiar. It carried mostly local news. Not long after our arrival, a picture of our family at a picnic, plates full of food, was splashed on the front page. It seemed absurd to me. Surely there was more significant news to report. However, it led to a fortunate connection.

After seeing our picture in the paper, another Latvian family, the Jaundalders, reached out to us. The couple had two teenage sons and had lived in the area for a little over a year. Their oldest son, Imants, just graduated from the local high school and was only a couple years younger than Elga and me. The family lived and worked on a farm just eight miles from town. A young and well-to-do bachelor farmer had sponsored them. Through the Jaundalders, we learned there were 12 other Latvian families in the area.

The Latvian festival of Jani, or St. John's Day, celebrating the summer solstice near the end of June, was approaching. The community in Sioux Falls planned a celebration. With our family's conflicting work schedules and no car, we couldn't attend. Fortunately, the local Latvian families also planned a party, holding it at a farm nearby. When the day arrived, someone offered to take us. When we arrived, all the trappings of the traditional festival surrounded us.

"Mother, Father, look!" Maija shouted, jumping up and down with excitement.

Men wearing crowns of oak leaf clusters readied the *pudele*, a tub of wood raised high on a pole, for the dusk to dawn bonfire. Single women with wreaths of flowers in their hair and older women with headscarves laid out a spread of traditional

Latvian breads, cheeses, and food on an oversized table. People filled their plates with pork and sauerkraut, cold meats, and smoked fish, and grabbed a drink. Latvian music played in the background on a record player while people sang traditional folk tunes at the top of their lungs and clinked their glasses. It felt like I was back in Riga.

I saw Oma flitting about the room from one group to another. Since we arrived, I hadn't seen her smiling and laughing so much. She was in her element, meeting new people while Maija played with other children who spoke Latvian. It was good to see them outside of our downtown apartment, breathing the fresh country air, and meeting new people.

We met other families, like us, who had fled Latvia, lived in the DP camps of Germany, and had come to the American midwest. One family invited us to their home in the coming weeks. Another family had recently started work at the hospital, and their daughter Verena was our age. Still, another Latvian woman and her son were coming to work at the hospital soon. Our family's circle of friends was growing.

I was excited to tell Karlis about our family's good fortune. I had even more good news to share.

June 26, 1950
Dearest Karlis,

> *Are you at your resettlement camp yet?*
> *The newspaper reported five foreign doctors are*
> *being accepted for internships at a Sioux Falls Hospital.*
> *Upon completion and passing the exam, they will*
> *receive a state medical license. There are opportunities*

for work in South Dakota's rural areas. Financial help is
available. You must arrive soon to take advantage of it.

All my love,
Biruta

The next day I received a message from Karlis. It was apparent our letters had crossed in the mail. In it, I read the worst news I could have ever imagined. Karlis' immigration papers had been held up because he had been a medic for the German army.

I stared at the words, re-reading them over and over until they blurred through my tears. I wailed and crumpled the letter in my hand. Elga came running when she heard my sobs. She took the ravaged message from me and read it.

Father, Mother, and Oma entered the room, wanting to know what the matter was. Elga told them, and they each tried consoling me. I wanted to be alone with my grief and ran to my room, throwing myself on my bed.

Through my weeping, I didn't hear the knock at our front door or the muffled voices of Father and Mother talking to someone. Reverend Abrahamson happened to stop by to check in on our family. A few minutes later, I heard a soft rapping at my door and Mother calling my name.

"Biruta, Reverend Abrahamson would like to speak to you. We told him about the letter from Karlis."

I mopped the tears from my cheeks, blew my nose, and took a quick look in the mirror. Red splotches covered my face. My eyes were puffy from crying. I took a deep breath and hesitated before opening the door for the Reverend.

"Biruta, I'm so sorry to hear your news. I know it's a great disappointment," he said in a calm voice, "but there is still hope. I've heard of similar situations and know a state senator who might be able to help. I can also write to the regional Lutheran Welfare offices. We must be patient, but I'm sure things can be sorted out."

Sniffling, I looked up at him at hearing there may be a ray of hope.

"Do you really think something can be done?" I sputtered.

Reverend Abrahamson took my hands into his.

"With hope and prayers, things may be put to right. I'll see what I can do."

Through my tear-stained face, I gave him a weak smile, thanked, and embraced him before he left the room. I wrote to Karlis at once about my conversation with the Reverend.

Work at the hospital kept me busy, and I tried not to dwell on the barriers to Karlis' arrival. It wasn't hard because I'd been assigned to one of the more violent wards. I was shocked by the foul language coming from some of the patients. At the least opportunity, they'd yell, "Damn you!" or harsher insults. One patient even preceded it with an "Alleluia!" Sometimes I felt cursed, but then there was another patient who liked me very much and said, "Shall I pray for you?" It made the difficult times bearable.

There were also pleasant days at the hospital. Every ward was preparing for the Fourth of July celebration. The better patients made red, white, and blue decorations and practiced parts for an Independence Day program. They told stories of fireworks and parades from happier times in their lives, and there was a sense of joy and excitement on the wards.

After work, Elga and I spent many of our days off with the young people we met at the St. John's Day celebration: Verena; Imants Jaundalders; and his friend, Apsitis. No one had a car or could drive, but the Jaundalders's sponsor, Roland Wright, volunteered to be our chauffeur. He was in his thirties and owned several farms. With little time to socialize, he enjoyed spending time with us.

During weekday evenings, Yankton was a typical sleepy rural town. However, on Saturday nights, the downtown exploded with activity. All the stores stayed open late into the evening. The main street was overrun with farmers, ranchers, and their families going to church, shopping for supplies, eating at the restaurants, or drinking at the bars.

On Saturday nights, there was hardly room to park a car. The six of us often went to the movies and afterward stopped at a local café for sodas to talk about the picture, our past week, or share the latest joke. Sometimes we went up to our family's apartment to play cards and listen to the radio.

At one of the movies, the documentary *Why Korea?* was shown before the main feature. Examples of powerful countries exploiting smaller ones flashed on the screen; Japan's expansionism, Mussolini walking into Ethiopia, Stalin taking over Finland, and Hitler marching into Poland.

I turned to look at those sitting around me in the theater and thought that, besides my small group of friends, few people had experienced war or an occupation like we had. Stalin trampled over the rights of innocent families in the Baltics, hiding his crimes, and the world knew little of it. Millions of families had been uprooted by the war. I thought about our home in Latvia and wept silently in the dark.

Father was also dismayed about his co-worker's disinterest in world events. When the local paper arrived at the hospital, he said the attendants usually reached for the comic section first and read nothing else. Unless someone had a family member serving in the military, people paid little attention to the Korean war. Two local Lithuanian men recently arrived to America had been drafted.

Discussing it at home that evening, Oma recalled an old German saying:

"Many a mother worries if her son will be called to war,
Many a sweet girl cries when her lover leaves." [13]

Father, Mother, Elga, and I worked at the hospital for six weeks before getting our first paychecks. Since we started in early June, we had been surviving on one advance from the hospital. To save money, Father and Mother thought about getting an employee apartment at the hospital, but none large enough for our family was available.

The family had many debts, but my parents felt we needed a car. A good used car costs $900 and old jalopies around $150. They bought a 1936 Dodge for $250. The sales pitch was that the car's motor was good because it only belonged to one family. Father bought it on credit.

After work, a friend took Father and me out to the countryside to teach us how to drive. From the beginning, something was wrong. A strange noise came from underneath the hood and the radiator boiled over. We almost didn't make it back to town to a repair shop. No one could say Americans were uncaring and selfish. Someone from the church loaned us the money to make the repairs.

Two weeks later, we drove out to the country for another driving lesson and ran out of gas. The gas gauge didn't function properly. At work, we were always told to wear a smile. Some days it was hard.

In the first week of August, we got our full July wages. Some debts were paid, leaving us enough money to get through the month. The car wasn't paid in full, but Father, Mother, Elga, and I drove it to work every day. We tried to conserve gas by coordinating our shifts at the hospital.

One day, the four of us left work, and just as we left the hospital gates, got hit by a car. All of us were severely shaken but unharmed. We were told the car could be repaired, and Father and Mother made the calculations. We'd only had the car a month, but they decided it wasn't worth fixing.

Since the accident, we had more visitors than ever. Some came to inquire about our health, and others to get to know us better. Some came giving advice and others because of nosiness. A gentleman from the church came over to warn us about insurance scams just as an agent knocked at our door to sell Father life insurance. Our church guest, an ardent Lutheran, recognized the agent from a Catholic agency. He told the agent that if Father needed a policy, he would buy it from a Lutheran and shut the door in the salesman's face. After they both left, the family laughed at the comedy of it all.

Another family from the church, the Rulons, were extremely helpful to our family. They were under the impression that Karlis was German. When they learned about Karlis' immigration difficulties and that he was Latvian, they were interested in assisting us. I was excited to tell Karlis.

August 29, 1950
Dearest Karlis,

Mr. Rulon has contacts at the IRO headquarters in Geneva. He sent me a copy of his letter asking for their help in speeding your immigration to the United States. This time, your name is spelled correctly. I am beginning to have hope that I may see you again soon.

All my love,
Biruta

CHAPTER 20

Delays and Developments

At the beginning of September, despite previous promises, Father and Mother had heard nothing further about being able to work as psychiatrists. They continued to work at the state hospital as aides.

Some immigrant physicians had been recently let go, so it was not for lack of openings. One doctor, a Ukrainian, hadn't learned enough English to pass the state medical examinations. Perhaps the hospital had lost confidence that refugee doctors could be licensed. Out of frustration, my parents renewed their efforts to find employment elsewhere, even if it meant relocating from Yankton. Reverend Abrahamson wasn't pleased about the idea.

Elga was unhappy with work at the state hospital as well. With Reverend Abrahamson's assistance, she signed up for entrance exams at a nursing school in Sioux Falls. She returned excited about the first-rate hospital facilities, the congenial nursing students, and the prospects of life in a bigger city.

On the exam itself, Elga struggled with English comprehension and worried if she had passed the five-hour timed test. She hoped they would take into consideration her recent immigrant status. After a few weeks, she was notified that she wasn't accepted into their nursing program. Disappointed, she started looking for other jobs. My parents and Elga were unhappy about their work, but I thought I could endure until Karlis arrived. Many days, it was difficult.

September 1, 1950
Dearest Karlis,

> *I am discouraged not only about my work at the state hospital, but also how immigrants are treated. I am scheduled away from my regular ward and given the least desirable assignments. There is an overall animosity toward foreigners, and even a protest occurred in a nearby town.*
>
> *Some workers at the hospital gossip and talk behind my back, spreading rumors. One co-worker thinks I'm already married because I wear my engagement band on my left hand. She says I'm collecting money to help my German husband come to America. The "nosy crow" doesn't know anything about us or the immigration process. You're not German, and all of us repay our expenses to our sponsors through our wages. Some days I feel no one here likes us, and I'm no longer sure this is the best place for us.*

> *All my love,*
> *Biruta*

I received more bad news. Reverend Abrahamson informed me that because of the delays in Karlis' arrival, the farmer in Minnesota canceled his sponsorship. I slumped forward into a chair, holding my head in my hands, and closed my eyes. I was so accustomed to disappointment that no tears came. Reverend Abrahamson tried to console me by wrapping his arms around my shoulders.

"There won't be a problem finding work for Karlis, but we need to find him another sponsor," he said.

I sat up, opened my eyes and nodded, steeling myself for another round of patience.

After Reverend Abrahamson left, Father had an idea.

"I'm going to talk to Mr. Jaundalders at the Wright farm. Roland Wright owns several farms. Perhaps he would consider sponsoring Karlis. It would be reasonable for him to ask for additional help."

My face brightened at the suggestion. The following day, Father talked to Mr. Jaundalders who thought Mr. Wright might be open to the idea. He agreed to drive someone from our family out to the farm to speak to him. However, one of us would need to present the proposal to Roland.

I looked at Father with pleading eyes, "Can you please ask him?"

"Biruta, you know Roland Wright better than I do and are in a better position to explain Karlis' situation," Father said. "Besides, Mother and I can't possibly miss any work to go out to see him. We're still holding out hope to work as psychiatrists and can't give the hospital any excuse to deny us."

"Yes, but I know Roland as a friend. This is business. Can someone at least go with me?"

"I'll go," Elga said.

"We'll come along too," Oma replied, speaking for herself and Maija. "We'd enjoy getting out of this apartment and seeing the countryside again."

Roland knew that Elga, my parents, and I worked at the state hospital and that I was engaged, but he knew little else. When our group was socializing, I rarely spoke about Karlis. The next day, Mr. Juanalders picked us up and drove us out to the farm. When we arrived, Roland was startled to see us.

"Hello, Elga and Biruta. Oma and Maija, what a pleasant surprise," he said. "To what do I owe this pleasure?"

"Biruta has something important to discuss with you," Elga said, nudging me forward. "Oma, Maija, and I came along for the ride."

"I don't know where to begin," I stammered, clearing my throat. "Well, you know I am engaged..." and I told Roland about Karlis' sponsorship problem.

"You've been so good to the Jaunalders, is there any possible way you'd consider sponsoring Karlis as well?"

When I finished, Roland sat for a moment, lost in his thoughts.

"Well, I do own several farms. I could ask for additional help, but Karlis is a doctor. He wouldn't really be working for me, right?"

"Yes," I sputtered. "You'd be his sponsor, but he plans to work at the hospital. There are always openings there."

"I see," Roland murmured stroking his chin. "I'd be taking on a lot of responsibility with little oversight. What if he didn't get a job at the hospital or ran into financial trouble, what then?"

"The four of us in our family have steady jobs. We'd take full responsibility. He could even stay with our family temporarily. You'd have no obligations other than to sign the sponsorship papers," I said, my throat tightening and tears brimming at the corners of my eyes. "You're our only hope."

"Well, if you put it that way," Roland grinned. "I guess I have no choice but to sign. Where are the papers?"

I threw myself into Roland's arms. "I can't thank you enough. We'll bring the papers out tomorrow. You'll never regret this!"

Mr. Jaundalders had been standing in the corner of the room and walked over to shake Roland's hand.

"You'll not be sorry. You know how hardworking us Latvians are," he beamed.

Then looking at me, he said, "We'll expect front row seats at your wedding and reception. We'll want to be the first to toast the new bride and groom."

"Of course," I blushed. I was beyond thrilled that Roland had been so accommodating.

Roland held his head high and thrust his shoulders back. He asked for us to wait a moment and then went outdoors. The rest of us stayed inside, visiting with the Jaundalders. Roland returned a few minutes later with a fresh chicken he had just butchered and handed it to Oma.

"This is for your family dinner tonight. I think the occasion calls for a celebration," he said, shoving his hands into his pockets and rocking back on the heels of his boots.

We returned to Roland's farm the next day to bring out the sponsorship forms he needed to sign. Afterward, I promptly took them to the post office and expedited them to the immigration offices.

The forms were returned a week later. They were outdated, and new ones were required, in duplicate this time. A church member drove us back to Roland's farm to start the process all over again. Nothing ever moved as quickly as I wanted.

There was some other good news. Elga applied and secured employment at the local Catholic hospital. She was so excited to leave her current job that she bought herself a new pair of white nurse's shoes. Encouraged by Elga's success, Father and Mother inquired about work there as well, but there were no physician positions available.

"It's probably just as well," Mother said. "The church wouldn't have approved of our working there anyway. As it is, I'm surprised no one has said anything about Elga's new job."

"It's maddening," Father grumbled, "to work as aides when we were promised physician status after a few weeks. It's been almost five months, and still, there's been no word. Isn't there more that we can do?"

"We've asked and continue to be told to be patient. Perhaps Reverend Abrahamson can put in a word for us," Mother replied.

The Reverend was happy to advocate for my parents, but still, he received no further commitment.

A week later, Mother got word that, on a trial basis, she could start doing physical examinations on the hospital wards. It gave my parents hope just as they were ready to give up. However, the offer wasn't extended to Father. He seemed happy for Mother, but around the apartment, his sloping shoulders and unusual silence betrayed what a blow this was for him. The next day, he enlisted the help of a private tutor at the local college to help with his English.

～～

With limited space and no yard, the downtown apartment no longer suited our family. The noise from the street, especially on the weekends, exasperated all of us. My parents looked for a house to rent and found one in a quieter, more residential area.

It was a small home with just five rooms: a kitchen, living room, three small bedrooms, and a bath. Mother wondered whether a piano would fit in the living room and if one could be found at a reasonable price. Its most significant asset, however, was the yard. Oma and Maija could finally escape outdoors to fresh air and open space.

Around the same time, the head nurse asked if I wanted to work the early morning shift. I would finish work by 2:00 p.m. and have the rest of the day to myself. We hadn't replaced the car, and my work hours differed from my parents. It had complicated our transportation issues. I decided to accept the early morning position and took a shared employee apartment at the hospital.

The women's employee apartments were on the third floor of the building with the marble staircase. Like the nursing dorms in Munich, no men were allowed on the floor. The room was like a hotel room with carpeting, two beds, two dressers with mirrors and chairs, and a rocking chair. It was large, with two big windows and a narrow balcony overlooking the gardens. From it, I could see farm fields in the distance. I liked the apartment and thought I would stay if I kept working this shift.

I shared the room with an office employee who didn't stay at the hospital on the weekends. Everyone on the floor kept their doors open so that anyone living there could drop for a visit. Some employees always complained about work, and at times, it became annoying. Nevertheless, listening and conversing with co-workers provided an excellent way to practice my English, and for the most part, I enjoyed it.

As I got to know the secretarial staff, I thought more about becoming an office worker. I bought a book to teach myself shorthand, and a church member lent me a typewriter to practice my typing skills. I sat down to type a letter to Karlis.

October 8, 1950
Dearest Karlis,

It's October. The days are growing shorter, and there's a crisp chill in the air. After work today, I sat on my balcony, loosely wrapped in a blanket. For some time, I observed the quiet beauty outdoors. The grass is still bright green, but the trees have turned spectacular shades of orange and yellow. A few tall, dark pine trees are scattered among them, accenting their colors. When the sun peeks out from behind the clouds, the trees become even more vibrant.
Fiery red bushes border the hospital property, framing the golden farm fields in the distance. The Farmer's Almanac predicts a cold and snowy winter. Flocks of loud honking geese fly south in their V formations against the setting sun. The view takes my breath away. I wish you were here with me to share this beautiful sight.

All my love,
Biruta

A few days later, I heard through my friend, Imants Jaundalders, that the resettlement people had questioned Roland about his ability to take on another immigrant worker when he already employed and sponsored a family. Roland reported that he owned several farms and assured the agency he could use an extra hand.

The senator who promised Reverend Abrahamson he would help Karlis through his immigration issues lost interest. Another senator agreed to follow up, but I worried about additional delays.

The following week, I received copies of Karlis' immigration paperwork sent to the IRO, coordinating his resettlement. My hopes were renewed, but still, I hadn't heard anything from Karlis and wrote to him.

October 19, 1950
Dearest Karlis,

> *Once you wrote that you hoped to get to the resettlement camp by October. Now it is passed the middle of October, and I hear nothing from you. What do you know about your immigration status?*

> *All my love,*
> *Biruta*

In November, our family heard that in the coming weeks, a Latvian minister was coming to our area. A church service and reception were planned near Roland's farm. Our family went to the service and met with him afterward. Through our conversation, we were astonished to learn Reverend Kiploks had been in Augustdorf DP camp with Karlis. I was thrilled to talk to someone who knew Karlis and understood our predicament.

During the social gathering, Reverend Kiploks overheard several of us talking about our plans to celebrate Latvian Independence Day on November 18th. Even though the country was currently not autonomous, Latvians in the free world still celebrated its original independence. A group of us planned a short history program about Latvia for the local radio station. Reverend Kiploks was impressed by our enthusiasm to teach others about Latvia and how we had become refugees.

On November 18th, about 30 Latvians crowded into our parents' home to listen to our pre-recorded radio broadcast. After the program, everyone complimented the young people on the excellent job we had done. Then the traditional festivities began.

People indulged in Latvian foods contributed by our guests for the occasion. Glasses were emptied and replenished. Throughout the evening, the mood became more jubilant. Patriotic speeches commemorating the homeland were made, and ancestral folksongs were sung. Many of the women wept openly, recalling former lives abandoned in Latvia. Hopes ran high that one day our country would again be free.

Days after our celebration, we learned that some of our church sponsors were offended that they hadn't been invited. In preparation for our national observance, the Latvian planners decided it would be for Latvians only.

~∗~

By December, our family had been working for six months. The temperature outside dropped to a minus 15 degrees. There were underground tunnels between the state hospital buildings. I was lucky that I lived on the grounds. Elga had to walk from our parents' house to her new job.

I was assigned to one of the most violent wards again. One patient started a fight with another patient, kicked a window out with her bare foot, and needed to be restrained. The icy wind blew snow into the room. I was frustrated. I would need to become a wrestler if I didn't get a black eye first.

The head nurse said she assigned me to the ward because she needed good workers to handle the violent patients. It only made me more angry. If I was so qualified, why didn't I get a higher wage? The whole incident made me wonder if I could hold out until Karlis arrived. What helped me endure was the kindness of others.

December 10, 1950
Dearest Karlis,

Reverend Abrahamson gave me a thick packet of copied letters sent by our friends to Senator Gurney, the Displaced Persons Committee in Washington, D.C., the Lutheran Resettlement Services, and the chief Visa Division of the American Consulate in Bremen, Germany.

I'm indebted to so many people who are trying to help us. I can't count the number of times I've been asked when you are coming. I want to know too!

All my love,
Biruta

While waiting for a resolution to Karlis' immigration difficulties, I needed to focus on something positive. Karlis and I planned to get married soon after he arrived. Unexpectedly, my parents were invited to a wedding of a co-worker's daughter. It gave me an opportunity to learn about traditional American weddings.

Some of the customs I found unusual. From the outset, my parents and I thought it impolite that wedding invitations suggested gifts for the bride and groom. In Latvia, gifts were more thoughtful and personal. When my parents returned from the wedding, they reported the bride was "given away" by her father, a tradition we thought archaic. In the Latvian culture, the bride and groom walked as a couple down the aisle. It signified the start of their new lives together. At the end of the Latvian ceremony, engagement bands were moved from the left hand to the right instead of exchanging new wedding rings.

After the service, my parents reported there was a reception in the basement of the church. Only wedding cake and coffee were served. In Latvia, the parents of the bride hosted a spread of traditional food and drink for close friends and family in their home. I wasn't sure I wanted to follow the American traditions. I liked the Latvian ones better.

I also filled my time by studying for an upcoming psychiatric aide exam. It was a national test that hadn't been given at our hospital before. It was challenging to learn the U.S. system of weights and measures. I couldn't believe Americans hadn't converted to the metric system. Frustrated, instead, I tackled the cross-stitch pillow I was making for Mother for Christmas. Later, I typed another letter to Senator Gurney.

The next day, I heard from Karlis. His message was the news I needed to lift my spirits and carry me through the holidays. Filled with excitement, I wrote back to him immediately.

December 19, 1950
My Dearest Karlis,

I received your letter and the good news that your resettlement process is starting. Finally, finally! I remember how it was when our family went through all the steps for immigration.

*I think about our last Christmas together at Augusdorf
and long to be with you again. But you are coming soon!
My Christmas wish is coming true!*

All my love,
Biruta

On December 24th, I worked an early shift at the hospital.
Afterward, I went to my parents' home to decorate their tree.
The family spent a quiet dinner at home and later went to the
11:00 p.m. Christmas Eve service at our sponsoring church.

It had been a long day. I struggled to keep my eyes open.
Instead of going back to my hospital apartment, I stayed
overnight at my parents. On Christmas Day, Elga and I played
with Maija and her new toys. Later, I helped my parents host
some Latvian friends in their home.

Latvians also celebrated the second day of Christmas. Our
family went to hear Reverend Kiploks at a Latvian church service.
His words of faith, hope, and love were the most meaningful
part of my Christmas. Nevertheless, during the rest of the week,
I grew melancholy, remembering my Christmas a year ago with
Karlis. I found myself wondering if he was at the resettlement
camp and if a departure date had been set. Someone from the
church had offered to drive me to the train station in Sioux City
when Karlis arrived. Yet when would that be?

I was scheduled to work at the hospital on New Year's Eve.
A dance was planned for the patients, and I helped decorate
for the party. At the celebration, I danced with the patients
and found it more enjoyable than I expected. When it was
over, I went to my parents, bringing balloons, noisemakers, and
confetti to Maija.

Soon after the New Year, another letter came from Karlis. He said he needed to meet again with the consulate officials in Bremen, Germany before he could go to the resettlement camp. I assumed he was there and had trouble understanding the delay. I shored up my patience once again, convincing myself that although the process was moving slowly, it was moving forward.

January 5, 1951
Dearest Karlis,

After your last letter, I pray that by now, you are finally at the Grohn resettlement camp.

All my love,
Biruta

❧

I focused again on work. The scores of the psychiatric aide exam I had taken before the holidays were recently posted. I hadn't noticed them until some co-workers came up to congratulate me. I received the top score and won the right to represent the hospital at a national competition in Washington, D.C. There was also a monetary reward.

I was proud of my achievement, but noticed some co-workers weren't happy. There was tension at the hospital about my winning the recognition. One aide who had worked at the hospital for over 10 years, placed third. She had always been frosty toward foreigners. A doctor who had always considered my parents equals now opposed my representing the hospital.

The next day, I was notified to go to the hospital superintendent's office. Every muscle in my body tensed as I crossed the courtyard to the main hospital building. I arrived at his office, announcing myself to his secretary. I sat down in the waiting area, clutching my hands to keep them from trembling.

When called, I walked in timidly into the superintendent's wood-paneled office. He sat behind his oversized desk in a tastefully appointed office with leather chairs and motioned for me to sit down. He cleared his throat to address me.

"Biruta, first of all, I want to congratulate you on your score on the psychiatric aide exam. I've also have heard reports of your exemplary work on the wards.

"However," he continued, "you haven't been here a year yet. The administration has decided it would be best to acknowledge a longer-term employee to represent our hospital in Washington, D.C. I hope you understand."

I dug my fingernails into the arms of the chair, and a flash of anger went through me. I had studied long and hard for the test and had worked the most difficult wards in the hospital. I deserved the recognition and shouldn't be denied. I drew in a deep breath and blew it out in a slow, steady stream.

At the same time, I thought to myself, I didn't want hard feelings with my co-workers. It would only draw more attention to myself.

"I see," I said quietly. "I'm sure you've considered what's best for the hospital, and I don't want to question your decision."

"Yes. Thank you, Biruta, for understanding," the superintendent said as he stood up.

I stood up as well. He put a hand on my shoulder, guiding me toward the door.

"And keep up the good work. We value good employees like you."

Later that day, the third-place aide who had worked at the hospital the longest was chosen to be the representative to Washington, D.C. and awarded the monetary prize. It wasn't fair, but I was satisfied to know that I had really won the honor. Nevertheless, I was proud to be among the first class of certified psychiatric aides in South Dakota. It was a milestone for the hospital. The local newspaper covered the story complete with pictures on the front page. I also got a raise. Overall, it meant little when I received Karlis' next letter.

January 8, 1951
Dear Karlis,

> *I'm heartbroken and depressed! I've received the worst news of my life! I have headaches from crying ever since I read your letter. It will take another two weeks to clear things up???*
>
> *I can't believe anything anymore. Everything possible has been tried. What else can be done? From the first of the year, Senator Gurney is no longer in office. Reverend Abrahamson and Mr. Rulon can do no more. Who can we depend on any longer?*
>
> *All my love,*
> *Biruta*

Karlis' difficulties in coming to America were not his alone. All Eastern European men forcibly drafted into the German army during the war were not allowed to enter the U.S. The Latvian ambassador, Mr. Feldmanis, and the Latvian newspaper, Laiks, encouraged all Latvians to petition President Truman. The President was considering a resolution allowing forced draftees to resettle here. My family and I wrote, adding to the dozens of letters we had already written.

In Karlis' letter, he also said that until his emigration status was cleared, he needed to earn an income. He signed up to be a doctor on an Italian ship taking refugees resettling to other countries.

"Damn the immigration authorities!" he wrote in his letter. "If the ship goes to New York, I will jump ship and take a taxi to South Dakota to be with you."

I met with a Lutheran Aid worker who regularly checked in with our family. When she asked me about Karlis, I shared what he wrote in the letter. Her face paled.

"Biruta, I know these months have been excruciating for the both of you, but please don't encourage Karlis to do anything rash. There could be severe consequences, including his never being allowed to come here if he enters illegally."

I knew what she said was true. I put down my impulses to encourage Karlis and prompted him to be patient and continue through the proper channels.

Several weeks passed without knowing what was happening. I was finding it hard to hold myself together. At last another letter arrived. Tearing it open and reading it, I smoldered with anger and frustration.

February 13, 1951
Dear Karlis,

> *Sausmas! Terrible! Australia! Thirty-five more days!*
> *I'm looking on a map. Your ship is going to the farthest corner*
> *of the earth away from me!*

> *All my love,*
> *Biruta*

The pain of not knowing when or if I would see Karlis again tore me part. However, I was concerned on the home front as well. Father was still working as a psychiatric aide. Reverend Abrahamson gave up pressing the issue with the hospital administration and turned it over to the Lutheran Aid worker. Father was humiliated and losing hope that he would ever work as a physician again.

On several occasions at home, I noticed Father brooding alone and talked to Mother.

"What do you hear about Father's position? The New Year has come and gone, and still, he hasn't been promoted. Why do you think they're holding him back?"

"I worry about him as well," Mother acknowledged, her face grim. "His professional skills are not lacking, but his heavy accent may be a hindrance. I'm planning to go to the hospital administration myself to find out what the problem is."

Mother went to the chief of staff the next day. Surprisingly, she was told Father could start working as a psychiatrist at the beginning of March. He would replace a German physician who was being been let go. I was thrilled when I heard the news. I wanted to give Father a good start and started going home in the evenings to help him with his pronunciation.

February flowed into March, and Karlis' job on the ship took him to Australia and Southeast Asia. I heard less frequently from him, only receiving letters when he could post them from a port. I stayed at my hospital apartment and saw less and less of my family. Both Father and Mother were full-time psychiatrists now working long hours. On my days off, I spent time with Elga, Verena, Imants, Apsitis, and Roland, but it was hard keeping my spirits up.

March 15, 1951
Dearest Karlis,

I don't know where to send my letters anymore. By the time this gets to Australia, you probably won't be there anymore.

All my love,
Biruta

In the first week of April, President Truman signed the order allowing Eastern European draftees to immigrate to the U.S. I was overjoyed. Soon after, a letter came from Karlis saying he was back in Germany and at the resettlement camp. It was hard to believe that all the hurdles for Karlis' immigration had finally been cleared.

April 12, 1951
My Dearest Karlis,

Hopefully, all this letter writing will end! From your letter, you should be here soon! You say there is a sailing to the U.S. on April 22nd. There is a Latvian gathering in Sioux Falls on May 6th. Wouldn't it be wonderful if we could go together!

Let me know when you're scheduled to arrive in Sioux City! I'll be there!

> *All my love,*
> *Biruta*

There were further delays, and Karlis did not make the April 22nd sailing. I was growing accustomed to the roller-coaster pattern of hope and despair. At the end of April, his arrival date was set. I hoped it would be the last time I would have to write to Karlis.

April 30, 1951
My Dearest Karlis,

Bon Voyage! I hope this letter reaches you before you leave. I will be waiting for you at the Sioux City train station!

> *All my love,*
> *Biruta*

Karlis was scheduled to arrive by train on May 19, 1951. It had been almost a year since our family had done the same. I couldn't believe he was actually coming.

With my work savings, I bought myself a pale, yellow sundress with a matching cape that covered my shoulders. I wanted to look my best and knew the color would accent my blue eyes and brunette hair.

On the morning of Karlis' arrival, I was at my parents' home. I put on my new dress, curled my hair, added a touch of lipstick, and walked out into my parents' living room.

"As they say in America, va-va-voom!" Elga said as I entered the room. "Karlis will melt when he sees you."

I blushed and was anxious to leave, asking my parents if they were ready to go. Father and Mother would accompany me to the train station. The car was already outside, waiting to take us to Sioux City.

We arrived at the station early. I went out to the platform while my parents agreed to wait inside. My stomach turned in knots as I saw the distant headlamp of Karlis' train approaching. It chugged into the station and stopped with a screeching halt.

The doors opened, and Karlis was one of the first to exit. His eyes scanned the platform. Upon seeing me, he ran, picked me up, and twirled me around in his customary greeting.

"Biruta, it's been a year. I'm here at last. You look wonderful!"

"You look wonderful yourself," I grinned.

"Are you sure?" Karlis asked with a look of concern. "I've been on a ship for six weeks with an abundance of Italian food. I've gained a little weight and was afraid you wouldn't have me anymore."

"Seriously, Karlis? I've been waiting too long to let go of you so easily," I laughed.

I grabbed his hand, pulling him toward the station and the waiting car. "Now, let's get going to Yankton. I have so much to show you."

❧

On June 2, 1951, exactly two weeks after his arrival, Karlis and I married at Trinity Lutheran Church in Yankton, South Dakota. Elga, of course, was my maid of honor and our friends Verena, Imants, and Apsitis rounded out our wedding party.

A small group of family, friends, and members of the church attended. Both Reverend Abrahamson and Reverend Kiploks presided over the ceremony. Karlis' sponsor, Roland Wright, and the Juanalders family had honorary seats at the front of the church to witness our wedding.

In the Latvian tradition, when the service began, Karlis and I walked down the aisle together. At the end of the ceremony, our rings were blessed, and we moved each other's engagement bands from the left hand to the right. Our wedding was consecrated.

Afterward, a reception was held in the basement of the church with members serving cake and coffee. Later, my parents hosted our close friends and sponsors to a traditional Latvian dinner at their home.

Karlis and I were officially man and wife. After escaping the occupations of Latvia and years of displacement after the war, finally we could go forward with our lives. Together in America, Karlis and I would build our new home.

Karlis and Biruta's Wedding Day,
June 2, 1951 and signed note from
Pastor, Reverend Abrahamson

Trinity Lutheran Church
Yankton, South Dakota
G. L. Abrahamson, Pastor
June 2, 1951

Epilogue

~~~

After their marriage, Biruta and Karlis lived and worked at the state hospital in Yankton for six months. They moved to Sioux Falls, where Karlis began a medical internship at McKennan Hospital, earning a small stipend while Biruta worked as a nurses' aide. In 1952, they welcomed a daughter, Lilita, and at the end of that year, Karlis obtained his state medical license.

The couple moved to Hosmer to provide medical services to the northcentral part of the state, an underserved rural area. Biruta worked beside Karlis as his receptionist, office manager, and nursing assistant. During the day, a local German woman took care of their one-year-old daughter. In 1953, a son was born, Sigurds, and in 1955, a daughter, Inese.

The family moved 40 miles east to Leola, a slightly larger town of 800 people, which had a 12-bed hospital. A fourth child, another daughter, Tamara, was born in 1958. When the hospital closed in 1966, the family moved east to the larger community of Aberdeen, where Karlis worked another 20 years before retiring in 1986.

Keeping up with Latvian traditions in sparsely populated rural South Dakota was challenging. Other Latvian families and physicians also immigrated to the central plains of

America. Despite being miles apart, the families made efforts to keep in contact. Every summer solstice, Latvians throughout the world celebrated *Jani* or St. John's Day and the Dakotas were no exception.

Several times a year, Biruta and Karlis' family drove five hours to Minneapolis, Minnesota, to visit Latvian friends and attend events there. Latvian organizations host concerts, folk dancing, and choral groups in the larger metropolitan areas. Regular social gatherings at Latvian meeting halls and churches continue to reinforce the culture. The family also often attended the biennial Latvian Song Festivals held in various major cities in the United States and Canada.

Biruta immigrated to the U.S with her family, but Karlis' father, step-mother, and four adult siblings remained in Latvia during and after WWII. Under Russian occupation, there was minimal contact between Karlis and his immediate family members, and letters, if received, were often censored.

In 1962, Karlis was notified that his father had died. It was the height of the cold war, and Karlis and his brother Alfreds, also residing in the U.S., could not attend their father's funeral in Latvia. After Gorbachev's policy of Glasnost in 1985, Soviet relations with the west softened.

In subsequent years, Karlis and Biruta made at least three different trips to Latvia. On their initial visit, Biruta met the rest of Karlis' siblings for the first time. Later, two of Karlis' sisters and other family members were able to travel from Latvia to the United States.

The fall of the Soviet Union in 1991 resulted in Latvia, Lithuania, and Estonia regaining their independence. With the support of NATO, the three Baltic states remain independent to this day but stay wary of Russian interference.

Karlis was also a noted Latvian author. He wrote *Balta Pils*, a book named after the refugee ship on which he worked while going to Australia and Indonesia before reuniting with Biruta. His novel is based on some of his personal experiences during and after WWII. He also penned two other novels, a book of essays about Latvian patriots, and two books of poetry in his native Latvian. In 2001, Karlis was recognized for his literary contributions to the country by the Latvian President, Vaira Vike-Freiberga.

Karlis lived his belief in love at first sight. He and Biruta were happily married for over 63 years. After Karlis' retirement, the couple divided their time between South Dakota and Florida and enjoyed world travel. Karlis died in 2015 at the age of 94. Biruta survived him and lived in South Dakota until her death in October 2020.

Drs. Hermanis Riesbergs and Elsa Riesbergs (Father and Mother) continued living and working as psychiatrists at the state hospital in Yankton for many years. Emma Treuman (Oma) lived with the family. While the Drs. Riesbergs worked, she watched Maija after school. In 1955, at the age of 74, Oma died of cancer. Oma always kept Opa's silver flute, and it still remains in the family today.

In 1960 at the age of 62, Dr. Hermanis Riesbergs had a massive heart attack and died. The family often wondered if the stress of restarting his career in a new country contributed to his death. While he worked as a doctor at the state hospital, Dr. Hermanis Riesbergs was well-liked and well respected by his co-workers and fellow physicians. After his unexpected death, employees of the state hospital commissioned his portrait painted. It hung for many years in the employee building at the state hospital.

Dr. Elsa Riesbergs continued working as a psychiatrist until she retired at the age of 72. During her lifetime, she was able to make several trips back to Latvia to visit family and friends. When the Soviets re-occupied Riga in 1944, private homes once again became property of the state. Oma's and Opa's Mezparks home was subdivided, and other families assigned to live there.

With Latvia's renewed independence in 1991, private property was restored to its original owners. Fortunately, the family retained their ownership papers throughout their displacement and immigration. Elsa reclaimed the property, and her goddaughter managed it in Latvia. The Mezparks property was ceded to her when Dr. Elsa Riesbergs died peacefully in 2005.

When Elsa celebrated her 100th birthday earlier in 2005, the local paper ran a story about her life. Sulli Rinne-Kelly, researching for her mother's (Marianne Rinne's) memoir, came across the article. Sulli was living in Canada, having moved there from Germany in 1955. She reached out and reconnected with Biruta and Elga, maintaining contact with them between 2005 to 2010.

Throughout the years, the three sisters, Biruta, Elga, and Maija, maintained close ties to each other and their respective families. Elga married a fellow Latvian, Raymond Norgello, whose family had immigrated to Sioux Falls. The couple both worked in the medical field, Elga as a registered nurse and her husband as a medical technologist. They raised two sons and a daughter, Erik, Aldis, and Melinda, in Yankton. Elga died at the age of 85 of heart complications just five days after Karlis' death in 2015. Elga's husband preceded her in death a few years earlier.

Maija, a retired social worker, presently resides in Florida. She and her husband, Roger Schiedel, who recently passed away, lived and worked the majority of their professional careers in Colorado Springs, and raised two sons, Tyler and Ari.

In 2007 Maija, along with Biruta and Karlis' four adult children, spouses, and nine young adult grandchildren, totaling almost 20 people, took a group excursion to Latvia to reconnect with extended family. At the time, Karlis' health prevented him and Biruta from traveling with them. With cell phones in hand, family members made calls to Biruta and Karlis in South Dakota while visiting paternal aunts, uncles, and cousins in Latvia. An emotional highlight of the trip was a special phone call placed to Biruta and Karlis from Riga. It was made while standing in front of Oma's and Opa's former Mezparks home.

Biruta's 90th birthday celebration with her adult children

Footnotes

1. "I Have a Dream" Martin Luther King, Jr.
   New York: Grosset, 1968.

2. Lane, Thomas, Pabriks, Artis, and Smith, David J.,
   The Baltic States: Estonia, Latvia, and Lithuania,
   Routledge, (2017), pp. 24, 32.

   "Soviet occupation of the Baltic states (1940)."
   Wikipedia, The Free Encyclopedia. Wikipedia, The Free
   Encyclopedia, 26 Jul. (2020). Web. 3 Aug. (2020).

3. Dunsdorfs, Edgars. *The Baltic Dilema*, Speller & Sons,
   New York, (1975), p. 61.

4. Ezergailis. (1996), p.239 (Wikipedia-Rumbala massacre)
   (1996) p. 70.

5. Hill, Alexander. *The Red Army and the Second World War.*
   December 24, 2016 (Wikipedia "The Battle of
   Stalingrad") p..80.

6. *Latvia*, "WWII in the Baltic Region", The Book Latvia,
   Inc., St. Charles, Illinois (1984) pp. 93, 201-202.

7. History.com, Yalta conference, (2009) p 135.
   "Yalta Conference Agreement, Declaration of
   A Liberated Europe," February 11, 1945, History and
   Public Policy Program Digital Archive, National Archives.
   Phttp://digitalarchive.wilsoncenter.org/document/116176

8. Cohen, G.D. ,'Between Relief and Politics: Refugee Humanitarianism in Occupied Germany 1945-1946' (2008) p. 160. Journal of Contemporary History, Vol. 43(3); pp. 437-449.

9. Kinnear, M. (2004) Woman of the World. Mary McGeachy and International Cooperation, University of Toronto: Toronto (2004) p. 173.

10. Von Fallersleben, August Heinrich Hoffman (lyrics), Mozart, Wolfgang Amadeus, (music), * "Sehhnsucht nach dem Fruhling," (1798-1874) p. 194.

11. Faithful, A. and Blagojevic, P. (Footnote 7, 8 & 10) (2014), p. 195. United Nations Relief & Rehabilitation Administration (UNRRA) & International Refugee Organization (IRO) in Museums Victoria Collections https://collections. museumvictoria.comau/articles/13618)

12. Lazarus, Emma. "The New Colossus." *Statue of Liberty*, New York, New York. (1883).

13. Pommers, Ansis, *Fisbachas Virsos 1945-1950*, Hoover Library Archives, Collection #2007C6, Stanford University, California. hoover.org/library-archives/collections

Additional Reading

Additional reading about life in northern Europe circa WWII:

Sepetys, Ruta, *Between Shades of Gray* (2011) Penguin Random House, LLC, New York.
    Synopsis: *A young girl and her Lithuanian family do not survive the Soviet raids in her country during WWII and are shipped across Russia in railroad boxcars to work camps in Siberia.* (Historical fiction).

Sepetys, Ruta, *Salt to the Sea* (2016) Penguin Random House, LLC, New York.
    Synopsis: *Four fictional characters from different parts of Europe flee the Soviet occupation in their respective countries. They converge at a Baltic seaport to board the historic ship, the Wilhelm Gustloff.* (Historical fiction).

Upite, Ruta (Author), Liepa, Rita (Translator) (1978) *Dear God, I Wanted to Live*, Gramatu Draugs, a division of the Latvian newspaper, Laiks, New York.
    Synopsis: *A fourteen-year old's diary is smuggled out of Latvia and depicts the depravity and suffering of her mother, herself, and two sisters in the slave labor camps of Siberia.* (Non-fiction).

Zarina, Lilija (Author), Dickson, Gunna (Translator), (2006) *The Red Fog – A Memoir of Life in the Soviet Union*. I Universe, Lincoln, Nebraska.
    Synopsis: *A young woman studies medicine at the University of Latvia and describes a of life of fear and political oppression under Soviet-occupied Latvia.* (Non-fiction).

Acknowledgements and Resources

First and foremost, I want to express my love and gratitude to my 90-year-old mother, Biruta, for her guidance in writing her story. Several years ago, she wrote *My Story*, a nine-page document for us, her children. In it, she recorded her recollections of growing up before, during, and after WWII. In 2018, she and I began enhancing the document to create her memoir.

The events in the story are fact-based. Details were gleaned from my mother's memory about events happening 70 and 80 years ago. When specifics weren't recalled, she encouraged me to use my imagination and then reviewed every written word. When I got something wrong, she corrected me. More than two years and hundreds of phone calls later, I think I captured the essence of her story.

The persons named in the book were actual people from my mother's life. Some minor character names weren't recalled. The dialogue is my invention, but the overall intention true. I'm blessed that my mother has been with me to guide me through this process. Her memory and patience, as always, has been enduring. It is with much love and respect that I'm privileged to write her story.

Erik Norgello, my cousin and Elga's son, is credited for the information about our early maternal family history. In 1999, he interviewed our grandmother, Dr. Elsa Riesbergs, when she was 94. He created the document *Riesberg Memories*. It was a record for his two daughters but was also shared with extended family members.

My father, Karlis, kept my mother's letters describing her first impressions and experiences in America. She transcribed excerpts from that correspondence, which formed the foundation of the last three chapters. The family documents, the letters, and my parents' oral history shaped Biruta's story.

My grandmother's copy of *Fisbachas Virsos 1945-1950*[13] compiled by Ansis Pommers, was a photographic reference for me. He was a former resident of Camp Fischbach, along with my mother's family. He captured life at the DP camp in a journal of maps, manuscripts, and photographs during the five years that Camp Fischbach existed. In one picture, my grandfather, Dr. Hermanis Riesbergs, and other staff members are shown in front of the camp hospital. In another, Biruta and Elga are with their high school class and teachers.

The illustrated book, *Latvia*[6], was another source of valuable information. It is a comprehensive written and pictorial representation of Latvia's geography, people, culture, history, government, and involvement in World War I and World War II. A section covers the "Night of Terror" that resulted in the massive deportations to slave camps in Siberia. Later, it describes the refugee flight from Latvia to other countries upon the Soviet re-occupation.

My mother's family was fortunate to have had a connection and the means to develop an escape plan as the Soviets returned. Countless other Latvians, Lithuanians, Estonians, and Poles were not so fortunate. A few sample stories are provided in the *Additional Reading List*. There are hundreds of other books that have been written about experiences during this harrowing time.

As a first-time writer, I quickly discovered, as many authors have, that it takes a village to create a book. The following have been some of my most valuable villagers.

Through a local writing class, I met another novice writer, Susan Lewallen. Discovering that we were almost neighbors, we spent countless hours together critiquing each other's writing. We also did a lot of laughing. I would highly recommend her novel, *Crossing Paths*, set in Tanzania. It is based on her twenty years of experience while living and working as an ophthalmologist in Africa.

My writer's group was also instrumental in helping me develop the first half of this book. It consisted of Candace Conradi, Carol Carr, Barb Chardi, and Gloria Johnston. Unfortunately, our bi-monthly group disbanded before the book was completed.

Glenna A. Bloemen wears many "hats" besides that of being my editor. Despite the distractions and challenges of the COVID-19 pandemic, Glenna contributed her invaluable expertise, comments, and support for this project. One of her other jobs is that of being a co-editor of the newsletter for *Publisher and Writers of San Diego*. The PWSD community also provided a wealth of information.

Thank-yous also go to Olga Singer for her sharp eye in designing the cover and interior of the book, Charles Hardes for his mapping skills, and my cousin Aldis Norgello for sharing family documents.

I couldn't have created this book without my husband, Gerry. He provided much needed technical support when my computer was behaving badly. He also stepped up to the plate, literally, with the development of his culinary skills. His support sustained me and gave me time to write this book.

Last but not least, I acknowledge two of the most important people in my life, my adult children: Charles and Elisa. Leaving their grandmother's story as a legacy for them inspired me to write it.

About the Author
Lilita Zvejnieks Hardes

A first-generation American, Lilita felt compelled to tell her mother's story. Lilita's retirement made returning to the joys of the written word possible. A Licensed Clinical Social Worker (LCSW) by profession, she was a therapist in the Milwaukee area for 36 years. Growing up in South Dakota and spending most of her adult life with her husband in Wisconsin, they moved to San Diego to be near their two adult children and their families.

www.lhardes.com

In Memoriam
Biruta Riesbergs Zvejnieks
January 1930 – October 2020

Over the last two and a half years, Biruta consulted, reviewed, and approved every chapter of her memoir with the author. In the month before Biruta's death, although fully alert, her health began to fail her. In the first days of October, Biruta, an avid reader, was personally given a proof copy of her book. She was thrilled with the result and spent an afternoon pouring over the pages. She died peacefully in her sleep the following day.

CPSIA information can be obtained
at www.ICGtesting.com
Printed in the USA
LVHW110004260121
677508LV00007B/413